DOMESTIC PEACE

DOMESTIC PEACE:
Quranic Guidance for Building Healthy Family Bonds

DR. ALI MOHAMED SALAH

1446/2025

LOOH PRESS LTD.

First Edition, First Print April 2024

PRINTED & DISTRIBUTED BY
Looh Press Ltd.
56 Lethbridge Close
Leicester, England. UK
www.LoohPress.com
LoohPress@gmail.com

CONTACT AUTHOR
Ali.Kuantan@gmail.com

A catalogue record of this title is available from the British Library.

COVER DESIGN & TYPESET
Kusmin (Looh Press)

ISBN
978-82-693677-0-6 Paperback

Waxaan Ku billaabi
Magaca Eebbe,
Naxariistaha,
Naxariista badan

CONTENTS

DEDICATION

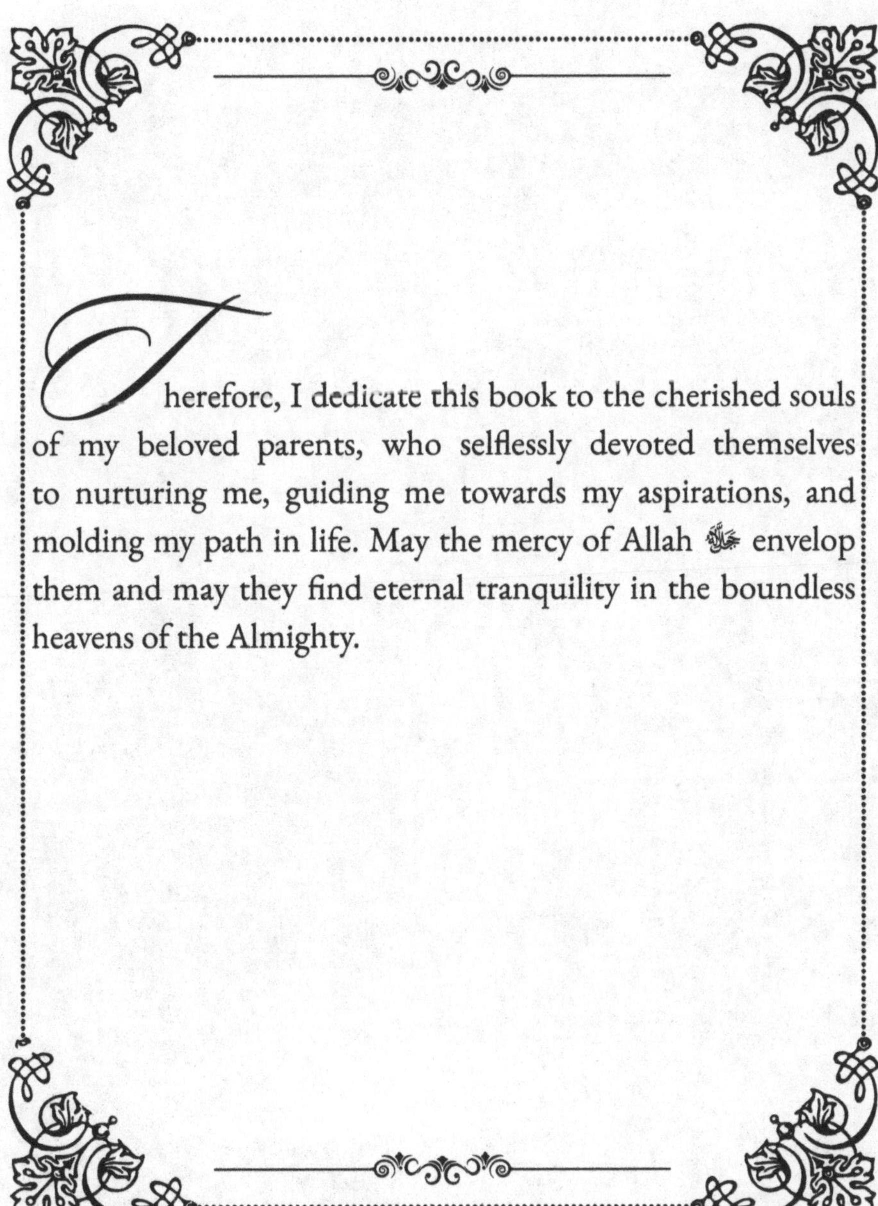

Therefore, I dedicate this book to the cherished souls of my beloved parents, who selflessly devoted themselves to nurturing me, guiding me towards my aspirations, and molding my path in life. May the mercy of Allah ﷻ envelop them and may they find eternal tranquility in the boundless heavens of the Almighty.

ACKNOWLEDGMENT

I extend my deepest gratitude to Allah ﷻ for His guidance and assistance throughout the completion of this writing endeavor. Without His unwavering support, this work would not have come to fruition.

I am sincerely thankful to all individuals who provided support and assistance during the writing process of my book. Their contributions, encouragement, and steadfast belief in my capabilities have been invaluable, and I am profoundly appreciative of their presence in my journey.

Foremost, I express my heartfelt appreciation to my family for their unconditional patience and understanding throughout this endeavor. Their unwavering support and willingness to sacrifice their own needs for my writing pursuits have been immeasurable, and I am forever grateful for their presence in my life.

Additionally, I extend special thanks to Mohamed Isak for his technical expertise and guidance, which played a pivotal role in shaping the content and structure of this book. His contributions, patience, and technical support are deeply appreciated.

To all who have contributed, regardless of the extent, in bringing this book to fruition, I extend my sincerest thanks. Your support has been invaluable, and I am genuinely humbled by your presence in my life.

With profound appreciation.

INTRODUCTION

Indeed, all praise and thanks are due to Allah ﷻ. We praise Him, we seek His assistance, we seek His forgiveness, and we seek His guidance. Whomsoever Allah ﷻ misguides, no one can guide, and whom Allah ﷻ guides, no one can misguide, and I bear witness that there is no one worthy of worship save Allah ﷻ, and Muhammad ﷺ is his final Messenger.

As a long-time resident of the Western world deeply engaged in Da'wa activities, I have had privileged access to the Muslim community, particularly its younger members, whom I have guided, instructed, and counseled in their personal affairs. In this context, I have witnessed a concerning trend: a staggering increase in divorce rates within the demographic I have interacted with. Families are crumbling, couples are separating, and familial bonds are disintegrating, seemingly without

substantial cause.

Upon closer examination, it becomes evident that the primary contributing factors to these familial breakdowns stem from a widespread ignorance of the fundamental marital teachings of Islam. These teachings, intended to guide Muslims through all facets of life, particularly family matters, offer invaluable wisdom aimed at benefiting individuals in both their temporal existence and the eternal realm of the hereafter.

In the context of the Western milieu, Imams, spiritual leaders, judges, and other community figures find themselves inundated with time constraints and busy schedules, preoccupied with mediating, arbitrating, and resolving family disputes. Regrettably, this often leaves little opportunity for comprehensive education and guidance on marital matters rooted in Islamic teachings.

It is disheartening to witness marital discord leading to the dissolution of unions over seemingly trivial issues that could be managed and mitigated with the application of wisdom and a deeper understanding of Quranic and Prophetic traditions.

The most tragic casualties of these marital failures are often the children, who find themselves deprived of the nurturing care and stability enjoyed by their peers from intact families. Recognizing this dire need for guidance and intervention, I present this book entitled "Domestic Peace: Quranic Guidance for Building Healthy Family Bonds."

This book endeavors to illuminate pathways and methodologies that can guide couples from conflict to concord, should they encounter challenges that threaten the continuity of their familial ties. Its overarching objective is to immerse readers in the spiritual and moral ambiance of the Quran and Sunnah, enabling them to draw pertinent lessons from these sacred and authoritative sources to enrich their marital relations and safeguard the integrity of their family units.

By embracing the teachings encapsulated within these pages, readers will be equipped with the tools necessary to navigate the complexities of marital life, fostering resilience, understanding, and harmony within their households. Through a synthesis of timeless wisdom and contemporary insights, this book aspires to serve as a beacon of hope and guidance for those traversing the tumultuous seas of marital discord.

Author:
Dr. Ali Mohamed Salah
30/3/2024

ABSTRACT

Indeed, all praise and thanks are due to Allah ﷻ. We praise Him, we seek His assistance, we seek His forgiveness, and we seek His guidance. Whomsoever Allah ﷻ misguides, no one can guide, and whom Allah ﷻ guide

This book delves into the moral responsibilities expected of spouses according to the teachings of the Quran and authentic Prophetic traditions. It aims to extract lessons from various Quranic verses, applying them to issues within marital and parent-child relationships. Additionally, it sheds light on the legal aspects of arbitrating conflicts within marriages.

Methodology

The methodology employed in this book entails a thorough collection of Quranic verses and relevant narrations, followed

by an examination of their relevance to contemporary challenges faced by the intended readership.

Objective

The primary goal of this book is to address the needs of newly married couples, particularly those raised in Western societies. It seeks to equip these individuals with the necessary guidance to navigate their marital journeys in accordance with Islamic principles. By addressing the lack of Islamic environment and education in their surroundings, the book aims to empower readers to uphold these principles effectively.

SECTION 1

SOCIAL MORALITY IN THE QURAN

1.0 MARRIAGE AND MORALS IN ISLAM

1.1 Importance of Marriage:

Marriage plays a profound role in shaping the morality of a society. It is not simply one of many social institutions but rather the most important and foundational moral institution in any society. The moral impact of marriage is so pervasive and essential that it often goes unnoticed, much like the beating of one's own heart. From an Islamic perspective:

A- Islam acknowledges the religious virtue, social necessity, and moral advantages of marriage. This is why marriage is considered a sacred duty, a moral safeguard, and a social commitment in Islam. As such, Islam encourages and invites those who are capable to enter into marriage, with a particular emphasis on the youth who are in dire need of it, even more so than other segments of society. Accordingly, the renowned companion, Ibnu Mas'ud, may Allah be pleased with him, related from the prophet ﷺ and said:

« كنا مع النبي صلى الله عليه وسلم شباباً لا نجد شيئاً، فقال: يا معشر الشباب من استطاع منكم الباءة فليتزوج، فإنه أغض للبصر وأحصن للفرج، ومن لم يستطع فعليه بالصوم فإنه له وجاء »

"We were with the Prophet ﷺ, young men who had nothing of wealth. So, the Messenger of Allah ﷺ said to us: "O young men, whoever among you can afford it, let him get married, for it is more effective in lowering the gaze and guarding one's chastity. And whoever cannot afford it should fast, for it will be a shield for him."[1]

B- Marriage attains true bliss and success when it is built upon religiosity, which serves as the foundation of morality, surpassing worldly gains and considerations. Islam regards marriage as a means of reducing crime within the community and addressing youth issues, provided that it adheres to Islam's criteria and moral standards. The Sunnah emphasizes the significance of marriage through two sayings, offering instructions and recommendations in this regard: Abu Huraira reported that the Prophet ﷺ said:

« إذا جاءكم من ترضون دينه وخلقه فزوجوه إلا تفعلوه تكن فتنة في الأرض وفساد كبير »

"If one whose character and religion pleases you comes to you (with a proposal), you should marry him (to your single woman). If you do not do so, there will be tribulations in the land and great corruption"[2].

Abu Huraira also narrated that the Prophet ﷺ said:

1. The hadeeth was narrated by al-Bukhaari (5066) and Muslims (1400).
2. Tirmidi, 1080

« تُنْكَحُ المَرْأَةُ لأَرْبَعٍ لِمَالِهَا وَلِحَسَبِهَا وَجَمَالِهَا وَلِدِينِهَا، فَاظْفَرْ بِذَاتِ الدِّينِ تَرِبَتْ يَدَاكَ »

"A woman is married for four things, i.e., her wealth, family status, beauty, and religion. So you should marry the religious woman, may your hand be besmeared with dust (otherwise) you will be a loser".[3]

A- Islam considers marriage a strong bond known as Mithaqun Ghaleez, a challenging obligation. It is a commitment to the dignified survival of the human race, fulfilling one's pleasure, and preserving one's deen. The believers' religious adherence and their commitment to Islamic teachings are demonstrated through marriage.

وَكَيْفَ تَأْخُذُونَهُۥ وَقَدْ أَفْضَىٰ بَعْضُكُمْ إِلَىٰ بَعْضٍ
وَأَخَذْنَ مِنكُم مِّيثَٰقًا غَلِيظًا ﴿٢١﴾

"And how could you take it while you have gone in unto each other and they have taken from you a solemn covenant?"[4]

The Quran states that guarding one's private parts and avoiding unlawful sexual contact with the opposite sex can only be afforded by a true believer and a fully devoted religious person. As stated in the Quran:

وَٱلَّذِينَ هُمْ لِفُرُوجِهِمْ حَٰفِظُونَ ﴿٥﴾
إِلَّا عَلَىٰٓ أَزْوَٰجِهِمْ أَوْ مَا مَلَكَتْ أَيْمَٰنُهُمْ فَإِنَّهُمْ غَيْرُ مَلُومِينَ ﴿٦﴾

3. Bukhari 5099 and Muslim 1466
4. An-Nisa', Ayah 20

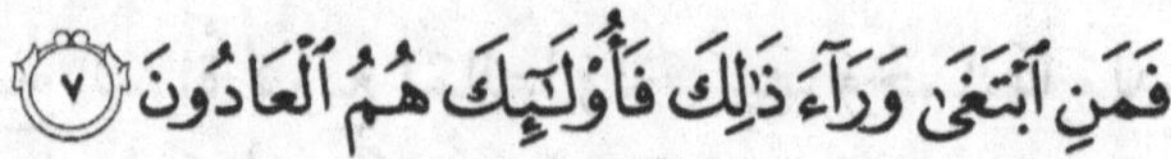

"And they who guard their private parts". "Except from their wives or those their right hands possess, for indeed, they will not be blamed -But whoever seeks beyond that, then those are the transgressors." [5]

Marriage also fulfills the purposes for which Allah ﷻ created natural sexual desires in human beings.

Imam Ibn Al-Qayyem, in his book At-Tibb An-Nabawi, highlighted the purposes of sex by stating that it was created to preserve and propagate the human race, expelling semen, fulfilling physical desires, and enjoying sexual pleasure. The Prophet ﷺ used to enjoy normal intimate relations with his wives, and he considered women and perfume dear to him in this world, as stated in a narration by Anas Bin Malik:

« حبب إلي من دنياكم الطيب والنساء »

"In your world, women and perfume have been made dear to me."[6]

Moreover, Ibnu Al-Qayyem added by saying: Sex is a means of maintaining good health, lowering the gaze, enabling self-control, and keeping away from prohibited things, and all of these benefits are achieved for both men and women.[7]

In Islam, the purpose of marriage goes beyond worldly gains. The guidelines and teachings of Islam emphasize that marriage

5. Al-Mu'minun, Ayah 5 – 7
6. Narrated by Ahmad 3/128 and An-Nasa'I 7/61.
7. At-Tibb An-Nabawi. Medicine of the Prophet page: 249.

is a religious duty that should be fulfilled to attain maximum righteousness. Islam encourages believers to prioritize religiosity and spirituality over material aspects when considering marriage.

Procreation of offspring in Islam is viewed as a means of increasing the number of Allah's servants on earth rather than solely seeking worldly advantages. Through marriage, a Muslim can draw closer to their Creator by fulfilling the responsibilities and obligations associated with marriage, such as demonstrating tolerance, patience, and other virtues. Marriage in Islam provides a means for emotional and sexual satisfaction, acts as a mechanism for reducing tension, facilitates legitimate procreation, promotes social placement, and fosters inter-family alliances and group solidarity. Most importantly, it offers opportunities for acts of worship (Ibadah) and the practice of piety.

In his article "The Morality of Marriage and the Transformative Power of Inclusion," Lynn D. Wardle argues that marriage plays a vital role in numerous ways in establishing the moral core, baseline, and standards for society. He cites several reasons he believes marriage is the most potent and crucial institution for generating morality in any society.

Firstly, marriage is a ubiquitous social institution that forms the cultural infrastructure of any society. It is a foundation upon which all surviving societies are built.

Secondly, marriage is the institution where most children are born and experience their earliest socialization, including forming moral ideals.

Thirdly, marriage is usually the family's foundation, the social unit where the earliest human socialization occurs, and the family's most successful and stable foundation.

Fourthly, in marriage and family, the individual acquires his core kinship identity, essential for not feeling like an outsider.

Fifthly, marriage and family are where most people learn about relationships and the morality of living in them.

Sixthly, marriage is the hub of the most connective experiences and the most transformative personal experiences for most people, making kin of strangers and bridging between generations and genders.

Seventhly, marriage is the site of some of the most critical and challenging steps in most individuals' moral development.

Eighthly, marriage is the institution with the most special connection with one of the most powerful and heavily stimulated human passions - sexual relations. Finally, **ninthly,** religion and marriage are closely linked conceptually, symbolically, practically, and often legally, with morality due to religion's direct or indirect influence.[8]

8. Wardle, Lynn D. "The Morality of Marriage and the Transformative Power of Inclusion" (September 1, 2008).

2.0 MORAL CODES AND GUIDELINES ON MARITAL HARMONY IN QURAN AND SUNNAH

The Quranic verses and prophetic narrations presented below explicitly and implicitly illustrate the moral objectives and wisdom behind marriage. These sacred texts provide guidelines that revolve around various moral themes, encapsulating Islam's perspective on marriage as an institution that contributes to the ethical fabric of societies.

2.1 Moral significance of verse 223 of surat al-Baqra:

(*Emphasizing Procreation, Chastity, and God-consciousness in Marriage*)

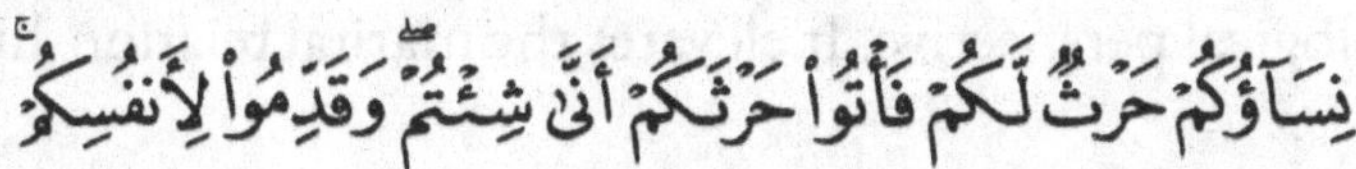

وَٱتَّقُواْ ٱللَّهَ وَٱعۡلَمُوٓاْ أَنَّكُم مُّلَٰقُوهُۗ وَبَشِّرِ ٱلۡمُؤۡمِنِينَ ٢٢٣

"Your wives are a place of sowing of seed for you, so come to your place of cultivation however you wish and put forth [righteousness] for yourselves. And fear Allah and know that you will meet Him. And give good tidings to the believers".[9]

In this verse, the importance of procreation is highlighted as a fundamental aspect of marriage, as it allows for the continuation of the human race. The fulfillment of natural sexual desires within the confines of marriage is considered essential in maintaining chastity and preserving moral standards, according to Islam.

The latter part of the verse, ***"And fear Allah and know that you will meet Him***," reminds spouses to remain conscious of Allah ﷻ and their accountability to Him. It underscores the need to maintain righteousness and spiritual connection while fulfilling their physical needs. This awareness helps believers adhere to the moral guidelines mentioned in the verse.

Islam acknowledges the significance of natural sexual desires and promotes a secure and harmonious environment within marriage to satisfy those needs. However, it emphasizes that the enjoyment of sexual satisfaction should be in accordance with Islamic teachings and principles.

"This verse not only addresses the physical aspects of the marital relationship but presents a comprehensive framework that sanctifies and contextualizes it within a moral, faith-based, and eschatological perspective. It elevates the marital relationship from

9. Al-Baqarah, Ayah 223

a purely physical act to an embodiment of faith, harmoniously combining the moral and sensual dimensions."[10]

In order to cultivate a spiritual atmosphere within marital relationships, Islam emphasizes the elevation of feelings from mere animalistic desires to a higher level of human connection. Islamic teachings highlight that the pursuit of pleasure in sexual relations should not be driven solely by carnal instincts. However, they should instead express love and affection between husband and wife. Islam introduces certain spiritual acts to be performed during sexual relations, such as making supplications (dua) and observing ritual purification (ghusl) afterward. It is important to note that other practices or customs surrounding sexual relations may vary based on cultural, traditional, or personal views.

Drawing from the verse mentioned above and the traditions of the Prophet, some etiquettes and manners can be derived, including:

A- Believers should have a sincere intention to engage in sexual relations solely for the sake of Allah so that they can be rewarded. And their intention should be the following:

Protecting oneself and one's wife from doing forbidden things. On the authority of Abu Dharr, the Messenger of Allah (ﷺ) said:

« وفي بضع أحدكم صدقة، قالوا: يا رسول الله، أيأتي أحدنا شهوته ويكون له فيها أجر؟ قال: »أرأيتم لو وضعها في حرام أكان عليه فيها وزر؟ فكذلك إذا وضعها في

10. The Moral Space of Marriage in The Holy Quran: "Relation between Spouses" from the Qura'nic Perspective and the Juristic Reading, Hend Mustafa, May 2018

الحلال كان له أجر »

"When any of you engages in sexual intercourse, there is a reward" (meaning, when he has intercourse with his wife). They said, "O Messenger of Allah, when any of us fulfills his desire, will he be rewarded? He (ﷺ) said: "Do you not see that if he were to do it unlawfully, he would be punished for that? So if he does it lawfully, he will be rewarded."[11]

Aiming to increase the number of the Muslim ummah to raise its status above other nations, our prophet ﷺ will take pride and honor in his people, outnumbering other prophets' people. He said on the authority of Anas Bin Malik:

« تزوجوا الودود الولود فإني مكاثر بكم الأمم »

"Marry women who are loving and very prolific, for I shall outnumber the people by you."

They should show total reliance on Him and seek His protection from satan as they start the action. On the authority of Ibnu Abbas the prophet ﷺ said:

« أَمَا لو أنَّ أحَدَهُمْ يقولُ حِينَ يَأْتي أهْلَهُ: باسْمِ اللَّهِ، اللَّهُمَّ جَنِّبْنِي الشَّيْطانَ، وجَنِّبِ الشَّيْطانَ ما رَزَقْتَنا، ثُمَّ قُدِّرَ بيْنَهُما في ذلكَ، أوْ قُضِيَ ولَدٌ؛ لَمْ يَضُرَّهُ شَيطانٌ أبَدًا »

"If anyone of you, when having sexual intercourse with his wife, says: "In the name of Allah. O Allah! Keep us away from Satan and keep Satan away from what You bestow on us (our children)."

The Prophet (ﷺ) also added by saying:

11. Muslim 1672

« فإن قضى الله بينهما ولدا ، لم يضره الشيطان أبدا»

"If Allah decrees that they should have a child, Satan will never harm him."[12]

The Hadith guides believers to be rewarded for their actions, even when seeking immediate pleasure and enjoyment. It emphasizes the importance of starting the action by mentioning Allah ﷻ and seeking His protection from the influence of Satan. The Prophet ﷺ taught us to recite the following supplication (Dua) before engaging in sexual relations:

This supplication serves as a means of seeking Allah's protection and blessing, acknowledging His authority over the act of procreation. It reinforces the spiritual dimension of sexual relations and highlights the belief that Allah's decree and protection are integral to the outcome of procreation. By reciting this supplication, believers express their reliance on Allah and their desire to involve Him in their intimate moments.

Kind words, playfulness, and affectionate gestures, including kisses, as a prelude to intercourse. Almighty Allah states in the Quran (interpretation of the meaning): "Your wives are a place of sowing of seed for you, so come to your place of cultivation however you wish and put forth [righteousness] for yourselves."[13]

Interpretations of this verse by most scholars, in light of sound narrations from the Prophet Muhammad ﷺ, suggest that the phrase "وَقَدِّمُوا لِأَنفُسِكُمْ" can be translated as "but do some good

12. Al-Bukhari 9/187.
13. Quran, Al-Baqarah 2:223.

act for your souls beforehand." This highlights the importance of engaging in foreplay and affectionate behavior that increases interest and creates a comfortable atmosphere.

It is important to note that the verse emphasizes that sexual relations should occur within the wife's vagina, as it is the natural place of procreation.

This indicates that the act of intercourse should be performed respectfully and appropriately while adhering to the prescribed boundaries.

Islam recognizes the significance of emotional and physical intimacy within the marital relationship by promoting kind words, playfulness, and affectionate gestures. These actions contribute to the overall well-being of both spouses, fostering a deeper connection and enhancing the enjoyment of sexual intimacy.

Jabir ibn `Abdullah (R.A) said:

« وعن جابر بن عبد الله رضي الله عنهما قال : كانت اليهود تقول : إذا أتى الرجل امرأته من دبرها في قبلها كان الولد أحول ! فنزلت : «نساؤكم حرث لكم فأتوا حرثكم أنى شئتم» فقال رسول الله صلى الله عليه وسلم «مقبلة ومدبرة إذا كان ذلك في الفرج» »

"The Jews used to say that if a man had intercourse with his wife in her vagina from behind, the child would have a squint." Then this verse was revealed: Your wives are a place of sowing of seed for you, so come to your place of cultivation however you wish and put forth [righteousness] for yourselves".[14]

So The Messenger of Allah ﷺ said: "From the front or the back, as long as it is in the vagina."[15]

Under any circumstances, it is important to clarify that in Islam, it is not permissible for a husband to engage in sexual intercourse with his wife in her back passage. The verse in question (Al-Baqarah 2:223) refers to the wife's vagina as the designated place for marital relations, as it is the natural and intended means of procreation. The term "place of 'tilth'" signifies the reproductive organ from which the hope of conceiving a child arises. This emphasizes the importance of preserving the sanctity and purpose of sexual intimacy within the marital bond while adhering to Islam's moral and ethical teachings. Furthermore, this evil act has been strictly prohibited also in the sunnah, "It is narrated from Khuzaymah bin Thābit that he said that the Prophet ﷺ said three times that:

« عَنْ خذيمه بن ثابت قَالَ: قَالَ رَسُولُ اللَّهِ صَلَّى اللَّهُ عَلَيْهِ وَسَلَّمَ: 'إِنَّ اللَّهَ لَا يَسْتَحْيِي مِنَ الْحَقِّ ثَلَاثَ مَرَّاتٍ لَا تَأْتُوا النِّسَاءَ فِي أَدْبَارِهِنّ »

'Indeed, Allāh (Most High) does not hesitate to mention the truth – do not have intercourse with women in their back passages.'"[16]

The Prophet ﷺ tells us in another Hadith that this action will cause the doer to be deprived of Allah's mercy, the meaning of the

14. Al-Baqarah: 223
15. Al-Bukhari 8/154 and Muslim 4/156 .
16. Sunan ibn Mājah, Hadīth 1924, vol 2, pg 450

curse mentioned in the Hadith.

« ملعون من يأتي النساء في محاشّهن : أي أدبارهن»

"He is cursed who has intercourse with women in their back passages."[17]

Some prophetic narrations not only warn against engaging in forbidden actions but also emphasize the severity of the consequences.

These narrations caution that the act of engaging in such forbidden actions, including specific sinful behaviors, may result in a state of being deprived of divine mercy and even lead to a weakening or loss of faith in the Holy Revelation. This serves as a strong admonition, emphasizing the gravity of these actions and their potentially detrimental effects on one's spiritual well-being. It underscores the importance of adhering to the teachings and guidance of the Holy Revelation to safeguard one's faith and maintain a righteous path. In this regard, the prophet ﷺ said:

« عَنْ أَبِي هُرَيْرَةَ، عَنِ النَّبِيِّ صَلَّى اللَّهُ عَلَيْهِ وَسَلَّمَ، قَالَ ' مَنْ أَتَى حَائِضًا أَوِ امْرَأَةً فِي دُبُرِهَا أَوْ كَاهِنًا، فَقَدْ كَفَرَ بِمَا أُنْزِلَ عَلَى مُحَمَّدٍ صَلَّى اللَّهُ عَلَيْهِ وَسَلَّمَ ' »

"On the authority of Abū Hurayrah, the Prophet of Allāh ﷺ said, 'The one who has intercourse with the menstruating woman, or has intercourse through her back passage or goes to a soothsayer, has disbelieved in what was revealed to the Prophet ﷺ.'"[18]

17. Ibnu Adiy 1/211. Sh. Albani graded it as an authentic narration in his book of Adab al-Ziff.
18. Sunan al-Tirmidhī, vol 1, pg 185, Hadīth 135

Islam forbids sexual intercourse with a woman while she is menstruating, considering it both unlawful and a major sin. This narration further highlights another prohibition related to intimate relations, explicitly addressing the act of engaging in intercourse during menstruation. This prohibition emphasizes respecting the natural biological process and observing the prescribed guidelines for intimate relations. It reminds individuals to exercise restraint and refrain from engaging in such acts during this specific period. Allah ﷻ says:

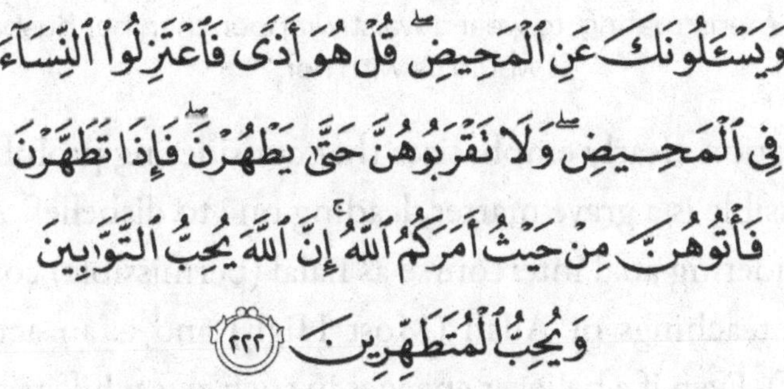

"And they ask you about menstruation. Say, "It is harm, so keep away from wives during menstruation. And do not approach them until they are pure. And when they have purified themselves, then come to them from where Allah has ordained for you. Indeed, Allah loves those who are constantly repentant and loves those who purify themselves." [19]

However, it is permissible for the husband to engage in other forms of physical intimacy and enjoy the company of his wife during her menstruation period without engaging in sexual intercourse. This allowance recognizes the importance of maintaining emotional closeness and affection between spouses, even during this time when sexual intercourse is prohibited. It encourages alternative ways of

19. Al-Baqarah, Ayah 222

expressing love and intimacy while adhering to the guidelines set forth by Islamic teachings. By abstaining from intercourse during menstruation, couples can still nurture their bond and strengthen their relationship through acts of love, companionship, and mutual support. According to a hadith by A'ishah (R.A), in which she said:

« كان رسول الله صلى الله عليه وسلم يأمر إحدانا إذا كانت حائضا أن تتزر ثم يضاجعها زوجها »

"The Messenger of Allah ﷺ would tell one of us, when she was menstruating, to wear a waist wrapper, then her husband would lie with her."[20]

The narration clearly emphasizes that considering prohibited acts as permissible is a grave matter, leading one to disbelief. Allowing and considering anal intercourse as halal (permissible) contradicts the clear teachings of Allah (Most High) and is an act of kufr (disbelief). Even if a believer engages in such acts while recognizing their prohibition, it still constitutes a major sin. It is essential to understand that, as Muslims, we must adhere to the principles set by Allah ﷻ and avoid actions that go against the teachings of Islam.

In addition to the religious perspective, engaging in anal intercourse goes against human beings' fitrah (natural inclination) and is repulsive to those with healthy human nature. It also deprives the woman of her rightful share of pleasure. Furthermore, the back passage is a place associated with impurity and filth, and various other reasons affirm the prohibition of such actions.

20. Agreed upon; Bukhari 300 and Muslim 293

Therefore, it is crucial for believers to respect and uphold the moral and ethical guidelines set by Islam, recognizing the wisdom behind these prohibitions and adhering to the teachings that promote physical and emotional well-being within the framework of righteousness and purity.

4- The intimate affairs between spouses should remain confidential and not be disclosed to others. It is impermissible for either spouse to divulge the private details of their marital life. In fact, this is considered one of the most reprehensible actions one can commit. So the Quran directs:

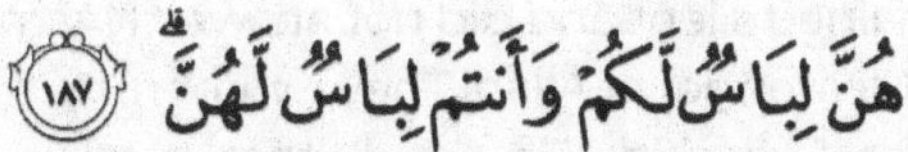

"They are clothing for you and you are clothing for them." [21]

The Prophet ﷺ also stated, on the authority of Abu Sa'id, by saying:

« إن من شر الناس منزلة عند الله يوم القيامة الرجل يفضي إلى امرأته وتفضي إليه ثم ينشر سرها »

"Among the most evil of people before Allah on the Day of Resurrection will be a man who comes to his wife and has intercourse with her, then he spreads her secrets."[22]

It was also reported from Asma' bint Yazid that she said that She was with the Prophet ﷺ, and men and women were sitting with him, and the Prophet ﷺ said,

21. Al-Baqarah, Ayah 187
22. Muslim 4/157.

« عن أسماء بنت يزيد رضي الله عنها، أنها كانت عند النبي ﷺ والرجال والنساء قعود عنده، فقال:
«لعل رجلًا يقول ما يفعل بأهله، ولعل امرأة تخبر بما فعلت مع زوجها؟» فأَرَمَّ القوم، فقلت: إي والله يا رسول الله، إنهم ليفعلون، و إنهن ليفعلن .فقال: »فلا تفعلوا، فإنما مثل ذلك مثل شيطان لقي شيطانة في طريق فغشيها والناس ينظرون.» »

"Would any man say what he did with his wife? Would any woman tell others what she did with her husband?" The people remained silent and did not answer. I [Asma'] said: "Yes, by Allah, O Messenger of Allah! They (women) do that, and they (men) do that." He said, "Do not do that. It is like a male devil meeting a female devil on the road and having intercourse with her while the people watch." [23]

2.2 MORAL CODES OF VERSES 2:228 OF AL-BAQARA AND 4:19 OF AL-NISA.

1- *The moral code emphasizes the principle of Ma'ruf (معروف) as the basis for reciprocal rights and obligations between spouses.*

2- *Ma'ruf encompasses kindness and mercy, promoting compassion and love rather than cruelty and hatred.*

For couples to establish a mutually respectful and morally upright relationship, Islam instructs them to adhere to the Quran's moral teachings in their interactions and dealings. By following these guidelines, couples can cultivate a harmonious and fulfilling

23. Abu Dawud 1/339. Al-bani: Adab Al-zifaf 143

marital bond that reflects Allah's mercy in their shared life In this, the Quran says:

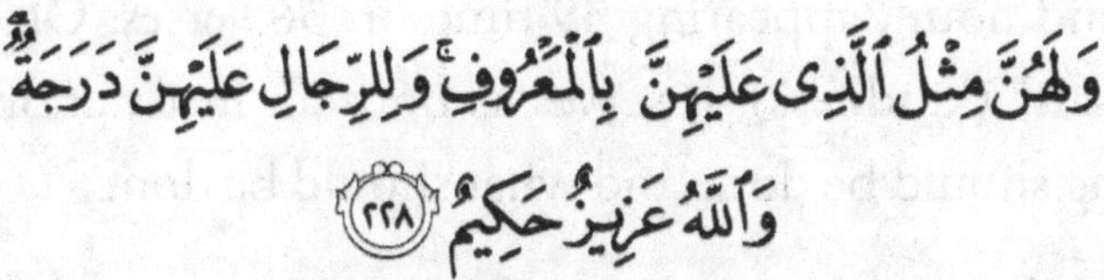

"And due to the wives is similar to what is expected of them, according to what is reasonable. But the men have a degree over them [in responsibility and authority]. And Allah is Exalted in Might and Wise".[24]

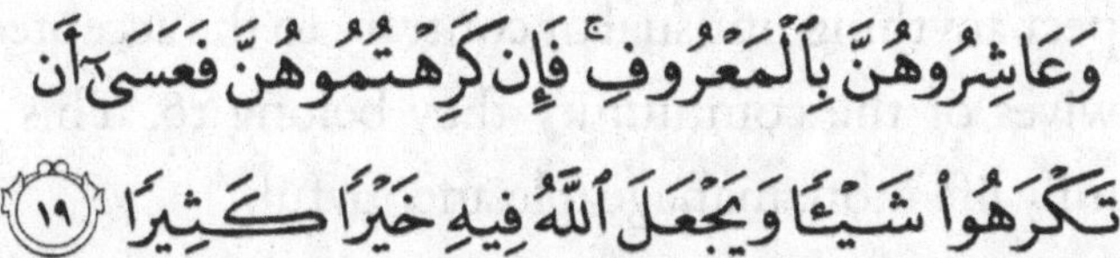

"And live with them in kindness. For if you dislike them - perhaps you dislike a thing and Allah makes therein much good".[25]

The foundation of a husband-wife relationship should be built upon the exchange of rights, mutual assistance, and a circle of love, affection, respect, and honor, encapsulated by the term "**Ma'ruf**." the Quranic verses emphasize that the rights and obligations between spouses should be rooted in reciprocity rather than strict equality. These verses recognize and highlight each spouse's distinct roles and functions, which are separate yet complementary.

"**Ma'ruf"** encompasses the entire concept of ethical behavior in the context of marriage. It represents the fundamental principles Islam sets forth for a shared life. The Quran repeatedly mentions this term, signifying its significance and importance in

24. Al-Baqarah, Ayah 228
25. An-Nisa', Ayah 19

various scenarios and situations. "**Ma'ruf**" appears in different grammatical cases as a definite and indefinite noun, adjective, adverb, and noun, appearing 39 times in 36 verses. Often paired with "ihsan" (kindness), it serves as both an instruction on how something should be done and what should be done.[26]

It is worth noting that the term "**Ma'ruf,**" in its various usages, primarily addresses men. It highlights the importance of men considering their wives' cultural norms and expectations when it comes to setting standards and making requests. Men are advised not to expect anything unusual or contrary to the accepted lifestyle of their wives or the community they belong to. This guidance makes family life more manageable and joyful.

While the phrase pertains to the general relationship between men and women, it explicitly emphasizes men's behavior, interactions, and overall conduct toward women rather than the other way around.

To gain a deeper understanding of the term "**Ma'ruf**" with the help of the Holy Quran, A. Kevin Reinhart cites a quote from Marshall G.S. Hodgson's book "The Venture of Islam: Conscience and History in a World Civilization." The quote highlights that the Quran does not need to outline every detail and method of action explicitly. It assumes that some aspects of goodness and righteousness are already known without specific revelation. The Quran acknowledges that individuals possess ordinary moral knowledge and urges them to act accordingly. It emphasizes performing actions with kindness and sincerity, adhering to the

26. "What We Know about Ma'ruf" by A. Kevin Reinhart in the Journal of Islamic Ethics

spirit of the law rather than merely its literal interpretation. In essence, the Quran not only imparts unique knowledge through revelation but also acknowledges the moral knowledge held by the Meccans, Medinans, and all Arabs who heard the Quran during the period from 612 to 632 CE.[27]

The moral space of marriage in the Holy Quran explores the interconnection between spouses from a Quranic perspective and a juristic interpretation. Therefore, "**Al-Ma'ruf**" defines every action recognized as good through intellectual understanding or legislative guidance. It signifies the concept of performing good deeds. Combined with these two meanings, "**Al-Ma'ruf**" is the foundational framework for marital relationships and broader family connections. It extends to the realm of relationships within the entire community of believers.[28]

The term "**Ma'ruf**" represents a lifestyle that aligns entirely with Allah's creation and desires. It encompasses a natural way of life that should be universally recognized and acknowledged, even by those who may not have knowledge of a holy book. It implies that Ma'ruf is a customary law established by Allah ﷻ, meaning that every community has its own understanding of Ma'ruf. However, it is essential to note that every Ma'ruf should be in accordance with the laws of Allah ﷻ.

In this context, the Quran recognizes that communal laws,

27. "The Venture of Islam: Conscience and History in a World Civilization" by Marshall G.S. Hodgson, quoted by A. Kevin Reinhart.
28. "The Moral Space of Marriage in The Holy Quran: 'Relation between Spouses' from the Qura'nic Perspective and the Juristic Reading" by Hend Mustafa.

customs, and habits that are not in contradiction with divine laws are considered Ma'ruf. This implies that practices and norms within a community are considered Ma'ruf as long as they are in harmony with the teachings and principles outlined by Allah ﷻ.

In general, Ma'ruf represents a standard of righteousness and goodness that transcends cultural and temporal boundaries, rooted in the laws and guidance of Allah ﷻ.

It is equally remarkable when the verse "ولهن مثل الذي عليهن بالمعروف" (And due to them [women] is similar to what is expected of them, according to what is reasonable) addresses the responsibility of women in such a manner. It establishes a balanced approach that considers both their obligations and rights. While the reciprocity of duties and rights is equal, the Quran introduces the condition of Ma'ruf, which encompasses the most comprehensive and inclusive term in Arabic, defining our treatment and interactions as spouses.

It is important to note that the term "**Ma'ruf**" is robust and inclusive, encompassing all the reciprocal rights and obligations within a marital relationship. The Quran does not elaborate on these rights, as they fall under the "**Ma'ruf**" umbrella, which is evident and known to everyone.

When examining the Quranic verses concerning the relationship between husbands and wives, one may notice a significant absence of a detailed list of specific "**Do's and Don'ts**" regarding their rights and interactions in their shared life. Unlike the extensive explanations Muslim scholars and jurists provided in their writings, the Quran does not explicitly lay out these rights and obligations comprehensively. This distinction in approach is because the Quran and Sunnah aim to convey their content and context lucidly and understandably, allowing readers to comprehend the principles and values underlying the marital relationship.

The concluding part of verse 19 of Al-Nisa states, "For if you dislike them - perhaps you dislike a thing, and Allah makes therein much good," highlights, in the context of "**Al-Ma'ruf**" and its implications, that marriage is founded upon affection and compassion. Therefore, it should be entered into through voluntary choice, creating an environment where mutual love, understanding, and compassion can flourish. In this regard, Islam advises husbands that even if they have moments of disliking their wives, those very wives may bring much goodness to their lives. Hence, the marriage bond should be cherished and not severed based on passing whims or fleeting emotions. Since marriage is a significant human institution, it should be approached with seriousness, and its longevity should not be subject to impulsive outbursts or superficial changes in sentiment.[29]

The prophet ﷺ summarizes the whole concept of "Ma'ruf" in three narrations: On the authority of Abuhurayra, the messenger ﷺ, said:

1- Messenger of Allah ﷺ said:

« لا يفرك مؤمن مؤمنة إن كرم منها خلقا رضي منها آخر أو قال غيره »

29. Fizilal-Al-Quran, pages 19-20.

"A believer must not hate (his wife) believing woman; if he dislikes one of her characteristics, he will be pleased with another."[30]

2- Abu Huraura also reported that the prophet ﷺ said:

« استوصوا بالنساء، فإن المرأة خلقت من ضلع، وإن أعوج شيء في الضلع أعلاه، فإن ذهبت تقيمه كسرته، وإن تركته لم يزل أعوج، فاستوصوا بالنساء »

"And I advise you to treat women kindly, for they are created from a rib, and the most crooked portion of the rib is its upper part; if you try to straighten it, it will break, and if you leave it, it will remain crooked, so I urge you to treat women kindly."[31]

3- Amr Bin Al-Ahwas Al-Jushamy said that the Messenger of Allah ﷺ said:

« الاَ وَاسْتَوْصُوا بالنِّسَاءِ خَيْرًا، فإنّمَا هُنّ عَوَانٌ عِنْدَكُمْ. أَلاَ وَإنّ لَكُمْ عَلَى نِسَائِكُمْ حَقّا، وَلِنِسَائِكُمْ عَلَيْكُمْ حَقا، فأَمّا حَقّكُمْ عَلَى نِسَائِكُمْ فلاَ يُوْطِئنَ فُرُشَكُمْ من تكْرَهُونَ، وَلا يَأْذَنّ في بُيُوتِكُمْ لِمَنْ تكرَهُونَ »

"O People, treat your women well and be kind to them; they are your partners and committed helpers. You indeed have certain rights concerning your women, but they also have right over you. And it is your right that they do not make friends with any one of whom you do not approve, as well as never to commit adultery".[32]

30. Muslim 1468.
31. Bukhari,114
32. Tirmidi 116

2.3 Moral codes of verses: 4:1 of surat an-nisa, 7:189 of al-araf, 16:72 of al-nahl, and 30:21 of al-rum.

These verses emphasize that familial relationships, integral to our human identity and the continuation of society, must be approached with morality and reverence, recognizing them as sacred bonds.

Surat Al-Nisa's introduction emphasizes key topics crucial for constructing a robust Islamic community and establishing a stable family structure, which serves as the core of a strong ummah. Additionally, the surah offers guidance to believers on how to unite their ranks and maintain their collective strength. The surah consistently underscores the significance of possessing a virtuous moral character in developing a resilient community. Moreover, it provides instructions on the rights and responsibilities of both spouses, enabling them to resolve their family disputes and cultivate a harmonious and well-regulated family life.

The surah, beginning with its sacred guidelines and directives, instructs us on how to establish a strong connection with Allah, the Creator, as well as our fellow human beings, Allah ﷻ says:

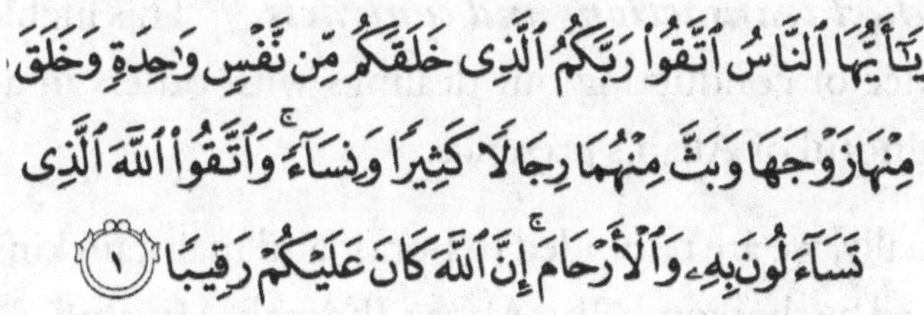

«O mankind, fear your Lord, who created you from one soul and created from it its mate and dispersed from both of them many men and women. And fear Allah, through whom you ask

> one another, and the wombs. Indeed Allah is ever, over you, an Observer.[33]

After commanding us to have Taqwa (consciousness and fear of Allah), Allah ﷻ reveals His divine plan that human existence on Earth begins with a single family, highlighting the family unit as the foundation of human life. Allah ﷻ states, "***and dispersed from both of them many men and women,***" signifying that from Adam and Hawwa (Eve), numerous men and women were created and distributed throughout the world in diverse forms, traits, colors, and languages. Ultimately, all of humanity will be gathered and returned to Allah ﷻ.

Allah ﷻ further instructs, "***And fear Allah, through whom you ask one another, and the wombs,***" reminding us to be mindful of Allah ﷻ in our interactions and transactions with others. According to some interpretations, this phrase implies that when seeking rights or making demands, we should invoke the name of Allah and acknowledge the ties of kinship. It is mentioned by scholars such as Ibrahim, Mujahid, and Al-Hasan.[34]

According to Ad-Dahhak, "***Fear Allah Whom you invoke when you conduct transactions and contracts.***"[35] This highlights the importance of conducting our dealings with others in a manner that is mindful of Allah's presence.

Additionally, we are reminded to honor and maintain kinship ties, symbolized by the womb. Ibn Abbas, Ikrimah, Mujahid, Al-Hasan,

33. An-Nisa" Ayah 1
34. At-Tabari 7:519
35. At-Tabari 7:518

Ad-Dahhak, Ar-Rabi, and others have emphasized the significance of not severing family ties but preserving and respecting them.[36]

In the prologue of Surah Al-Nisa in his book "Fi Zilal Al-Quran," Sayyid Qutb engages in a comprehensive discussion. Initially, he highlights the historical mistreatment and deprivation of women's rights in pre-Islamic societies. This sets the backdrop for understanding the societal context in which women existed during that era.

Qutub observes that the low status attributed to women in those societies had a detrimental impact on the foundational structure of families. The rules governing adoption and alliances often clashed with the bonds of kinship, leading to confusion and instability. Furthermore, chaotic relationships between men and women and within families were prevalent due to the prevalence of illicit relationships and societal norms at the time.

These factors contributed to an environment marked by disarray and disharmony. Qutb's analysis sheds light on the societal challenges faced during that period, providing insight into the importance of the Quranic guidance in rectifying these issues.[37]

In response to the prevailing oppressive treatment of women during that time, Islam emerged as a transformative force, elevating their status and granting them their rightful rights. This significant shift, which took place 1400 years ago, can be considered a revolutionary step in recognizing and valuing women's contributions and roles. Islam emphasizes the celebration of the inherent differences

36. At-Tabari 521-522
37. Sayyid Qutb, "Fi Zilal Al-Quran," Surah Al-Nisa, Page 6)

between men and women, acknowledging the diverse abilities and responsibilities that arise from their distinct genders. This acknowledgment is rooted in the understanding that Allah's creation encompasses a remarkable range of variations. No two individuals are identical, as evidenced by the multitude of variations in physical attributes, personalities, behaviors, skills, concerns, and functions. This diversity serves as a testament to the boundless power of Allah ﷻ, the Creator, who designed humankind with such incredible variation.[38]

However, it is essential to note that the differences between males and females, particularly in their roles and capabilities, should not be used as a means to exclude or deny rights to either gender. In the context of marital life, these differences exist within the boundaries of human ethics. Although they represent a form of distinction, they ultimately reflect a unity of nature and origin. Both males and females have been created from the same soul, and the Qur'an refers to them using the same term: "a mate" or "a spouse."[39]

As mentioned in the noble verse, the initial distinction between males and females serves the purpose of attraction, convergence, procreation, and the concept of "acquaintance" as described in the Qur'an. Through this concept, all things are created from the integration of two different spouses, ensuring the continuation of life's cycle and the ongoing movement of the cosmic wheel until it reaches its predetermined conclusion.[40]

38. Ibid Page 20
39. "The Moral Space of Marriage in The Holy Quran: 'Relation between Spouses' from the Qura'nic Perspective and the Juristic Reading" by Hend Mustafa)
40. ibid

The Qur'an's remarkable perfection becomes evident once again as we delve into the verses that constitute the moral code section of this discourse. Upon reflection, these verses eloquently convey the profound truth within Islam about the creation of Eve/Hawwa from Adam, emphasizing the interconnectedness and complementary nature of men and women. The Qur'an implicitly, rationally, and convincingly portrays the relationship between man and woman as that of a root and a branch. Just as a branch relies on its root for sustenance, and the root relies on the branch for growth and expression, so too do men and women depend on each other.

The Qur'an highlights how Allah ﷻ has instilled within the couple a profound sense of mutual need and how, through their union, they complete one another's imperfections and fulfill each other's needs. This divine design signifies the essential role of both genders in perpetuating human existence and the eternal cycle of procreation.

These verses resonate with the deeper truths of human existence, affirming the importance of unity, harmony, and interdependence between men and women. The Qur'an beautifully captures the intricacies of this relationship, underscoring the divine wisdom behind the creation of Eve as a partner and companion for Adam.

Through this profound understanding, Islam acknowledges the inherent value and significance of both men and women in the grand tapestry of creation. Allah ﷻ said:

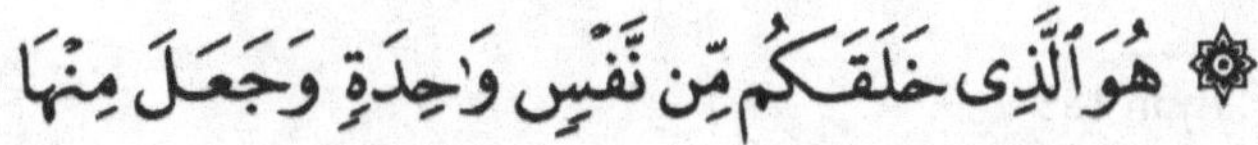

زَوْجَهَا لِيَسْكُنَ إِلَيْهَا فَلَمَّا تَغَشَّىٰهَا حَمَلَتْ حَمْلًا خَفِيفًا
فَمَرَّتْ بِهِۦ فَلَمَّآ أَثْقَلَت دَّعَوَا ٱللَّهَ رَبَّهُمَا لَئِنْ ءَاتَيْتَنَا صَٰلِحًا
لَّنَكُونَنَّ مِنَ ٱلشَّٰكِرِينَ ﴿١٨٩﴾

"It is He who created you from one soul and created from it its mate that he might dwell in security with her. And when he covers her, she carries a light burden and continues therein. And when it becomes heavy, they both invoke Allah, their Lord, "If You should give us a good [child], we will surely be among the grateful." [41]

وَٱللَّهُ جَعَلَ لَكُم مِّنْ أَنفُسِكُمْ أَزْوَٰجًا وَجَعَلَ لَكُم مِّنْ
أَزْوَٰجِكُم بَنِينَ وَحَفَدَةً وَرَزَقَكُم مِّنَ ٱلطَّيِّبَٰتِ
أَفَبِٱلْبَٰطِلِ يُؤْمِنُونَ وَبِنِعْمَتِ ٱللَّهِ هُمْ يَكْفُرُونَ ﴿٧٢﴾

"And Allah has made for you from yourselves mates and has made for you from your mates sons and grandchildren and has provided for you from the good things. Then in falsehood do they believe and in the favor of Allah they disbelieve" [42]

B- Verse 21 of Al-rum and 74 of Al-furqan " The moral ingredients of marriage; love, mercy, tranquility, and caring"

وَمِنْ ءَايَٰتِهِۦٓ أَنْ خَلَقَ لَكُم مِّنْ أَنفُسِكُمْ أَزْوَٰجًا لِّتَسْكُنُوٓا۟
إِلَيْهَا وَجَعَلَ بَيْنَكُم مَّوَدَّةً وَرَحْمَةً إِنَّ فِى ذَٰلِكَ
لَءَايَٰتٍ لِّقَوْمٍ يَتَفَكَّرُونَ ﴿٢١﴾

41. Al-A'raf, Ayah 189
42. An-Nahl, Ayah 72

> "And of His signs is that He created for you from yourselves mates that you may find tranquillity in them; and He placed between you affection and mercy. Indeed, in that are signs for a people who give thought." [43]

Verse 21 of Al-Rum clearly and confidently outlines the purposes and objectives of marriage. It acknowledges the deep emotional and instinctual bonds between a husband and wife as divine signs of Allah's greatness and countless blessings. While marriage serves as a means to fulfill one's physical needs in a dignified manner, it emphasizes that this is not its sole purpose or justification.

These verses, categorized under the moral code section, shed light on additional aims and fundamental principles that form the solid foundation of marital relationships. They highlight the importance of tranquility, love, and mercy as essential pillars that sustain the existence and flourishing of a marriage. These pillars epitomize the essence of care and compassion within the marital bond.

These three pillars serve as a moral equilibrium, guiding spouses through the various stages of their marital journey. From the inception of their union, symbolized by the planting of the first seed, to the later stages of their lives as they age together, each word—tranquility, love, and mercy—holds significance, offering guidance and support that aligns with the unique demands and circumstances of each phase of married life.

The first moral pillar of marriage is "**Tranquility**." It is a state that arises when a man and a woman, driven by needs more urgent

43. Al-Rum, 21

than hunger and thirst, long for each other. In this situation, both individuals feel a distinct emptiness that can only be filled through their union, as prescribed by divine laws, namely marriage. Through marriage, loneliness gives way to companionship, confusion gives way to stability, and longing and anxiety are replaced by tranquility and reassurance.

The term "لتسكنوا إليها" (translated as "finding tranquility") encapsulates the essence of marriage, representing the fundamental reason why Allah ﷻ created man and woman as spouses for one another. The root of the first Arabic word in the verse, "sakan," signifies a state of rest, quiet, calmness, and being unruffled, appeased, allayed, or motionless. This term highlights the motive behind marriage, emphasizing the deep need for tranquility that can only be fulfilled through the union of husband and wife.[44]

The second moral pillar of marriage is "**Love**," represented by the Arabic term "**mawaddah**." In the Qur'an and al-Hadith, this term is synonymous with "**wud**" and "**hub**." Commentators and linguists have differing opinions regarding the nuances between "**al-wudd**" and "**al-ḥubb**." Some suggest that "**al-mawaddah**" signifies the pinnacle of "al-maḥabbah." In contrast, others argue that "al-maḥabbah" is the more general term and "**al-mawaddah**" is more specific, indicating a natural inclination accompanied by affection. However, there are also views stating that "**al-maḥabbah**" is more specific and "**al-mawaddah**" is more general, encompassing love or a sense of longing. Some even consider them

44. Sadaf Faruq: An article titled "Two Important Rules for a Blissful Marriage" (22/8/2018),

complete synonyms.

Al-'Askarī supports the distinction between the two words, stating that "al-ḥubb" applies when love is dictated by wisdom and the natural disposition of the soul, while "**al-wudd**" is used solely when the soul is naturally inclined towards love. This can be observed when one says, "I love so-and-so and have affection for them" or "I love prayer," without using "al-wudd" to express the same sentiment.[45]

The terms "**Hub**" and "mawaddah" carry similar meanings to "**love**," but they are often used in different contexts based on the strength or degree of love involved. However, it is important to note that both terms refer to love, and the difference between them is rather subtle. "**Hub**" is often associated with the emotional aspect of love, particularly in the initial stages of attraction when one may not yet profoundly know the person. On the other hand, "**mawaddah**" is more connected to the practical side of one's behavior and attitude toward others. It represents a rational love that extends beyond emotions, especially in how one deals and interacts with everyone.

In discussing the different kinds of love within a person, it is mentioned that there are two aspects: the basic emotion of the concupiscible appetite, which is self-love driven by what benefits oneself, and the higher form of love rooted in the will, which is benevolence or willing the good of another for their own sake. These two kinds of love align with the concepts of "**Hub**" and "**mawaddah**." The first kind of love corresponds to the emotional

45. Al-furuuq Al-luquwiyya, p. 121

feeling of love, while the second kind pertains to the rational aspect of love.

Since a marital relationship is intended to be eternal and unbreakable, it is essential to undertake whatever sustains and preserves it, ensuring its success. This is where "**mawaddah**" comes into play, fitting perfectly in this second relationship stage. The verse mentioned describes how the marital relationship evolves over time, gradually transforming from embodying "**mawaddah**" (affection, love) to becoming a paradigm of "rahmah" (mercy). [46]

Lastly, the third moral pillar is Mercy, characterized by kindness, compassion, and care. It involves a willingness to forgive, overlook mistakes, and demonstrate understanding and tolerance. In the context of marriage, mercy plays a crucial role in maintaining harmony and preventing conflicts. It fosters forgiveness and contributes to establishing a strong and resilient relationship.

The balance between "**mawaddah**" (love) and mercy is vital in a marital relationship, fostering mutual understanding, love, and compassion. It serves as the foundation for a solid and healthy marriage and is considered one of the essential virtues in Islam.

Al-Rahmah, or "**Mercy,**" represents the final stage of the spouses' long marriage journey. It encompasses the phase when they may no longer be able to fully care for or fulfill each other's needs. Despite the challenges posed by time and life circumstances, they continue to treat one another with love, respect, and mercy. Rahma becomes the harvest season for what they have planted and

46. Sadaf Faruq, ibid.

nurtured throughout their relationship.

By upholding these moral pillars and cultivating qualities of love and mercy, along with cooperation and consultation, couples can create an environment that fosters tranquility, comfort, and peace of mind within their home.

The particular order in which these words appear in the Quranic verse holds special significance as it emphasizes the gradual transformation that occurs in the spousal relationship over time, influenced by the dynamics of age and experience.[47]

Interestingly, while exploring the explanation of this verse, one might draw an analogy between the structure of the marital relationship and the construction of a building. In building construction, four pillars are necessary to provide the structure with firmness and distribute the weight from the ceiling. Without these pillars, the building cannot stand on its own. It leads to a question as to why the Quran only mentions three pillars in the marriage structure, excluding the fourth pillar, which could have been the "pillar of rights" if it were explicitly referenced. The best answer lies with Allah ﷻ, as He knows best, and it could be attributed to one or both of the following reasons:

A. The pillar of "**rights**" may not be absent but rather intertwined and coupled with the main pillars of "**Al-mawaddah**" and "**Al-Rahma**." Love acts as a constant reminder of these rights. Where there is love and affection between the spouses, they naturally recognize and fulfill each other's reciprocal rights.

47. Ibid

B. As mentioned earlier, the concept of "**Ma'ruf**" encompasses all the reciprocal rights that arise in a marital relationship. Due to its inclusive nature, it carries a connotation of conferring and magnanimity. Where there is goodness and kindness (**Ma'ruf**), there is always a sense of caring, responsibility, and God-consciousness (Taqwa), ensuring rights are fulfilled.

These explanations highlight the comprehensive nature of the moral pillars in marriage, where love, mercy, and the concept of Ma'ruf encompass and inherently address the rights and responsibilities within the relationship.

The mutual family caring is what appears in the following verse of surat al-furqan:

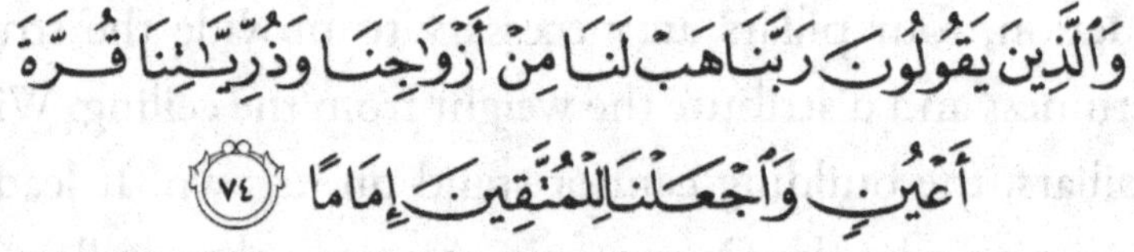

"And those who say, "Our Lord, grant us from among our wives and offspring comfort to our eyes and make us an example for the righteous." [48]

The verse tells us how caring the spouse is for one another and their offspring and that they are concerned about attaining comfort within the household. Moreover, the verse indicates how tranquility constitutes the foundation of stabled and blissful life; only when tranquility and comfort are granted can people prosper and progress in their world. Enjoying tranquility paves the way to worshiping Allah ﷻ and performing one's duty in this world for

48. Al-Furqan, Ayah 74

the success of the hereafter. Becoming genuinely righteous is how one can qualify to be a role model for other believers; the wisdom behind them asking Allah ﷻ to elevate them to be an example for the other believer.

The verse tells us how caring the spouse is for one another and their offspring and that they are concerned about attaining comfort within the household. Moreover, the verse indicates how tranquility constitutes the foundation of stabled and blissful life; only when tranquility and comfort are granted can people prosper and progress in their world. Enjoying tranquility paves the way to worshiping Allah ﷻ and performing one's duty in this world for the success of the hereafter. Becoming genuinely righteous is how one can qualify to be a role model for other believers; the wisdom behind them asking Allah ﷻ to elevate them to be an example for the other believer.

3.0 MARITAL CONFLICT RESOLUTION: MORAL GUIDELINES

Exploring Marital Harmony: Islamic Perspectives:

In previous discussions, we delved into the topic of marital harmony, examining Quranic passages, prophetic traditions, commentaries, and scholarly interpretations to shed light on its juristic dimensions. Islam greatly emphasizes fostering a tranquil and blissful marital life, recognizing the family's pivotal role in building a strong and harmonious society. The teachings of Islam emphasize the values of love, affection, mercy, and tranquility as essential components of a well-established and harmonious family relationship.

Islam's concern for marital harmony and conflict resolution is evident through the significant number of Quranic verses and authentic narrations dedicated to this subject. This demonstrates that these teachings go beyond mere directives to marry but also seek to promote sustainable and solid marital bonds characterized by harmony and minimal conflict.

Conflicts inevitably arise in any relationship, given the unpredictable nature of life and the challenges it presents. Spouses, being intimately connected, are particularly susceptible to conflicts and disagreements stemming from various sources and reasons. Islam acknowledges this reality and provides guidance and strategies to create a nurturing environment that mitigates discord and disharmony within marital relationships.

Islam offers a comprehensive approach to addressing conflicts, encompassing techniques to prevent conflicts from escalating and strategies for effectively resolving them when they do occur. These teachings encompass not only marital relationships but also general interpersonal interactions.

In Islam, we are encouraged to adopt techniques that promote harmonious relationships and prevent conflicts. These include effective communication, patience, forgiveness, empathy, and understanding. By adhering to these principles, individuals can cultivate a peaceful atmosphere within their relationships and avoid unnecessary conflicts.

Islam emphasizes the importance of upholding justice and fairness in resolving conflicts, ensuring that the rights and concerns of all parties involved are acknowledged and addressed. Moreover, Islam provides specific strategies for conflict resolution when disagreements do arise. These strategies encourage open dialogue, active listening, seeking mediation, and embracing compromise.

Individuals, by adhering to these Islamic teachings, can navigate conflicts within their marital relationships and maintain a healthy and harmonious bond.

The guidance provided by Islam is a roadmap for creating and sustaining lasting peace and tranquility within families and society as a whole.

A- MORAL GUIDELINES OF VERSES 34,35 and128 OF SURAT AL-NISA:

- Marital authority, financial obligation, internal conflict resolution (*mutual reconciliation*), external conflict resolution (*arbitration procedures*)

As mentioned earlier, the Quranic components for marital stability offer believers essential factors for maintaining a long-lasting and harmonious marriage, promoting longevity and unity between couples while preventing unnecessary family breakdowns and divorces. By examining verse 34 of Surah An-Nisa, we can observe its focused ethical approach in addressing the root causes of conflict and providing strategies for resolution through recognizing each spouse's role and responsibilities.

From the context of the verse, it becomes apparent that marital power dynamics, financial obligations, and trust issues are often the primary sources of marital conflict. Quran says:

ٱلرِّجَالُ قَوَّٰمُونَ عَلَى ٱلنِّسَآءِ بِمَا فَضَّلَ ٱللَّهُ بَعْضَهُمْ عَلَىٰ

بَعۡضٖ وَبِمَآ أَنفَقُواْ مِنۡ أَمۡوَٰلِهِمۡۚ فَٱلصَّٰلِحَٰتُ قَٰنِتَٰتٌ
حَٰفِظَٰتٞ لِّلۡغَيۡبِ بِمَا حَفِظَ ٱللَّهُۚ وَٱلَّٰتِي تَخَافُونَ نُشُوزَهُنَّ
فَعِظُوهُنَّ وَٱهۡجُرُوهُنَّ فِي ٱلۡمَضَاجِعِ وَٱضۡرِبُوهُنَّۖ فَإِنۡ
أَطَعۡنَكُمۡ فَلَا تَبۡغُواْ عَلَيۡهِنَّ سَبِيلًاۗ إِنَّ ٱللَّهَ كَانَ عَلِيّٗا
كَبِيرٗا ﴿٣٤﴾

وَإِنۡ خِفۡتُمۡ شِقَاقَ بَيۡنِهِمَا فَٱبۡعَثُواْ حَكَمٗا مِّنۡ أَهۡلِهِۦ وَحَكَمٗا
مِّنۡ أَهۡلِهَآ إِن يُرِيدَآ إِصۡلَٰحٗا يُوَفِّقِ ٱللَّهُ بَيۡنَهُمَآۗ إِنَّ ٱللَّهَ كَانَ
عَلِيمًا خَبِيرٗا ﴿٣٥﴾

"Men are in charge of women by [right of] what Allah has given one over the other and what they spend [for maintenance] from their wealth. So righteous women are devoutly obedient, guarding in [the husband's] absence what Allah would have them guard. But those [wives] from whom you fear arrogance - [first] advise them; [then if they persist], forsake them in bed; and [finally], strike them. But if they obey you [once more], seek no means against them. Indeed, Allah is ever Exalted and Grand. [49]

"And if you fear dissension between the two, send an arbitrator from his people and an arbitrator from her people. If they both desire reconciliation, Allah will cause it between them. Indeed, Allah is ever Knowing and Acquainted [with all things". [50]

The guidelines for conflict resolution continue in another section of the same chapter, Al-Nisa. Allah ﷻ says:

49. An-Nisa', Ayah 34
50. An-Nisa', Ayah 35

وَإِنِ ٱمْرَأَةٌ خَافَتْ مِنۢ بَعْلِهَا نُشُوزًا أَوْ إِعْرَاضًا فَلَا جُنَاحَ عَلَيْهِمَآ
أَن يُصْلِحَا بَيْنَهُمَا صُلْحًا ۚ وَٱلصُّلْحُ خَيْرٌ ۗ وَأُحْضِرَتِ ٱلْأَنفُسُ ٱلشُّحَّ ۚ
وَإِن تُحْسِنُوا۟ وَتَتَّقُوا۟ فَإِنَّ ٱللَّهَ كَانَ بِمَا تَعْمَلُونَ خَبِيرًا ﴿١٢٨﴾

"And if a woman fears from her husband contempt or evasion, there is no sin upon them if they make terms of settlement between them - and settlement is best. And present in [human] souls is stinginess. But if you do good and fear Allah - then indeed Allah is ever, with what you do, Acquainted".[51]

3.1 Marital authority (al-qawwamah)

Financial obligations: Verse 34 of Surah Al-Nisa addresses a common question when discussing marital issues:

Who should take on the leadership role within the marriage?

1- The concept of "Al-Qawamah" in the Quran and the interpretations of Quran commentators.

The Quranic verse asserts that men are assigned leadership roles within the marital relationship, highlighting the importance of having a leader and authority figure. This assignment should not be misunderstood as endorsing patriarchal dominance or suppressing women's rights. Upon its arrival, Islam challenged and dismantled such oppressive concepts that denied women their rights based solely on their perceived weakness. However, it is essential to acknowledge that men and women are not identical in their physical and biological attributes. These inherent differences may lead to variations in roles, capacities, and abilities, which can

51. An-Nisa', Ayah 128

influence their responsibilities within the marital framework.

The Prophet Muhammad ﷺ recognized these differences and assigned specific roles and tasks to each family member based on their capabilities. He said:

« عن ابن عمر رضي الله عنهما ، قال: سمعت رسول الله صلى الله عليه وسلم يقول: «كلكم رَاعٍ، وكلكم مسؤول عن رَعِيَّتِهِ: والأمير رَاعٍ، والرجل رَاعٍ على أهل بيته، والمرأة رَاعِيَةٌ على بيت زوجها وولده، فكلكم رَاعٍ، وكلكم مسؤول عن رَعِيَّتِهِ.» »

> "Every one of you is a shepherd and is responsible for his flock. The leader of people is a guardian and is responsible for his subjects. **A man is the guardian of his family and he is responsible for them.** A woman is the guardian of her husband's home and his children and is responsible for them."[52]

The narration emphasizes that wives also have domestic responsibilities in accordance with their abilities and capacities, ensuring that both spouses share the same boat and that no one is left behind. It is important to recognize that men and women, by their very nature as human beings, are equal in their humanity. This equality is not only inherent but also genetic.

In addition to their role as guardians, men are tasked with providing financial support for their wives, even in cases where women are financially independent or wealthy. This financial responsibility is part of the concept of Al-qawwamah mentioned

52. Bukhari 853 and Muslim 1829.

in verse 34 of Surah Al-Nisa. Al-qawwamah entails taking care of, protecting, supporting, and maintaining the interests of one's spouse, particularly in financial matters.

To gain a deeper understanding of the meaning and wisdom behind the Arabic word used in the Quranic text, let us refer to the following quotations from reliable sources of Tafseer:

According to Ibn Kathir, men are described as the protectors and maintainers of women, which signifies their role as leaders who have authority over women and are responsible for guiding and disciplining them if necessary.[53]

Al-Bagawi states that men are in charge of women's interests and affairs and have the right to discipline them. [54]

Al-Baydawi explains that men assume the leadership role of being in charge of their wives and caring for them[55]

In light of these interpretations, the principle of Al-qawwamah primarily implies financial responsibility, which is why husbands are entrusted with the leadership of the household. Additionally, a clear statement in the prophetic tradition emphasizes that husbands are financially responsible for their wives.

The prophet ﷺ, as reported by Ai'sha, said:

« دخلت هند بنت عتبة، امرأة أبي سفيان، على رسول الله ﷺ. فقالت: يا رسول الله! إن أبا سفيان رجل شحيح. لا

53. Tafsir Ibn Kathir, 1/653.
54. Tafsir al-Bagawi, 2/206.
55. Tafsir al-Baydawi, 2/184.

يعطيني من النفقة ما يكفيني ويكفي بني. إلا ما أخذت من ماله بغير علمه. فهل علي في ذلك من جناح؟ فقال رسول الله ﷺ «خذي من ماله بالمعروف، ما يكفيك ويكفي بنيك»».

"Hind bint 'Utbah, the wife of Abu Sufyaan, entered upon the Messenger of Allaah ﷺ and said, 'O Messenger of Allaah, Abu Sufyaan is a stingy man who does not spend enough on me and my children, except for what I take from his wealth without his knowledge. Is there any sin on me for doing that?' The Messenger of Allaah ﷺ said, **'Take from his wealth on a reasonable basis, only what is sufficient for you and your children.'**[56]**.**

Islam, with its just principles, views the family unit as a collective endeavor where no individual, whether the husband, wife, children, or others, is inherently superior or entitled to unfair treatment. Islam does not condone husbands oppressing their wives or denying them their rights under the pretext of exercising Qawaamah. These rights should align with the concept of justice within the local and contemporary context. The term **"Ma'ruf"** signifies this understanding, emphasizing the importance of treating one another with kindness, fairness, and respect within the marital relationship.

3.2 The concept of alqawamah in judaism (men's authority over women)

When issues of women, their rights, power (qawwamah), and their restrictive elements in society are discussed, some non-Muslims are always in favor of harboring the stereotyping view

56. Narrated by al-Bukhaari, 5049; Muslim, 1714

of labeling Islam as a patriarchal religion; because it stems from a patriarchal society in their view. Although that biased view is a dominating perception within the West but through unbiased study, one discovers that this immature view could apply to other religions and societies more than it is to Islam; the most restrictive elements towards women can be found first in Judaism in the Old Testament than in Christianity.

However, the issue of Al-qawwama, beating women, which will also be covered in pages of this chapter to come, in the discourse comparative topics with other religions, will unveil the reality that is not accessible to most people.

Concerning the issue of Al-qawwamah at hand, the Hebrew Bible clearly states that men should rule women over. According to Judaism, men have authority over women in the household, so she is supposed to show complete submission to the husband in all his orders and what he dictates lest she gets punished for failing. -Comparing.[57]

In Genesis 3:16, God says to women: "I will greatly increase your pangs in childbearing; in pain, you shall bring forth children, yet your desire shall be for your husband, and he shall rule over you."[58]

3.3 The concept of alqawamah in christianity (men's authority over women)

Christianity, Like Judaism, endorses the view that men should rule over women in all areas of society. In the teachings of

57. wife-beating" in Judaism, Christianity, Hinduism, Buddhism, and Islam: Muslim skeptic, August 7, 2022.
58. Genesis 3:16

Christianity, only men are entitled to be religious authorities. Just as a woman cannot become a rabbi in Judaism, she cannot become a priest according to traditional Christian teaching. Male religious authority is emphasized in the New Testament.[59]

In First Corinthians 11:3, Paul states: “But I want you to understand that Christ is the head of every man, and the husband is the head of his wife, and God is the head of Christ.”[60] In First Timothy 2:11 through 14, Paul states: “Let a woman learn in silence with full submission. I permit no woman to teach or to have authority over a man; she is to keep silent. For Adam was formed first, then Eve; 14 and Adam was not deceived, but the woman was deceived and became a transgressor.”[61]

Christian scripture also affirms that husbands have authority over wives. This Christian view is based on the Hebrew Bible or the Old Testament. As noted above, the Hebrew Bible asserts that women are to be ruled over by their husbands.[62]

The New Testament affirms that husbands have authority over wives and compares the husband to God, asserting that the husband’s authority is like God’s.[63] In the Bible, Paul speaks directly to women: “Wives, be subject to your husbands as you are to the Lord. For the husband is the head of the wife just as Christ is the head of the church, the body of which he is the Savior. Just as the church is subject to Christ, so also wives ought to be, in everything, to

59. Ibid
60. First Corinthians 11:3
61. First Timothy 2:11
62. ibid
63. ibid

their husbands."[64]

The Hebrew Bible also refers to the husband as "Ba'al," which means lord and owner. This term implies that the husband is the lord and owner of his wife.[65]

64. Ephesians 5:22-24
65. Ibid

4.0 INTERNAL CONFLICT RESOLUTION

(MUTUAL RECONCILIATION AND RESOLUTION)

Allah ﷻ says:

وَٱلَّٰتِي تَخَافُونَ نُشُوزَهُنَّ فَعِظُوهُنَّ وَٱهْجُرُوهُنَّ فِي ٱلْمَضَاجِعِ وَٱضْرِبُوهُنَّ فَإِنْ أَطَعْنَكُمْ فَلَا تَبْغُوا۟ عَلَيْهِنَّ سَبِيلًا إِنَّ ٱللَّهَ كَانَ عَلِيًّا كَبِيرًا ٣٤

But those [wives] from whom you fear arrogance - [first] advise them; [then if they persist], forsake them in bed; and [finally], strike them. But if they obey you [once more], seek no means against them. Indeed, Allah is ever Exalted and Grand.[66]

The occurrence of marital conflicts and disputes is an undeniable

66. An-Nisa"', Ayah 34.

reality, as disagreements can arise between spouses regardless of their compatibility. Just like any other human being, Muslim couples are not immune to such conflicts.

Recognizing the need to resolve conflicts is crucial for couples to address the existing problems. Ignoring conflicts in their early stages often worsens the situation, leading it to spiral out of control.

In the Quran, the verb "**خوف**" (**fear**) is used, which signifies anticipation, noticing, or a strong suspicion that something is amiss in the marital relationship. This serves as a call for believers to take immediate action to resolve the problem.[67]

Verse 35 of Surat Al-Nisa directs our attention to these situations within our families. The urgency emphasized in the Quranic verse highlights the importance of timely efforts to address and resolve disputes for the preservation of the marital relationship. Allah commands us to promptly seek a resolution by appointing arbitrators from both sides of the family.

Furthermore, the verb "**خوف**" (**fear**) is reiterated in verse 128 of Al-Nisa, where it states that if a woman fears contempt or avoidance from her husband, there is no sin upon them if they seek settlement and reconciliation. This verse encourages wives to take proactive steps, either independently or through arbitration, to prevent marital problems or address the behavior of overbearing husbands. It emphasizes the role of the wife in addressing issues before they escalate beyond control.

Therefore, the facts mentioned above illustrate the comprehensive

67. Al-Bagawi, vol:1, page:613

nature of the Islamic discourse on marriage, as depicted in the Quran and its paradigm for fostering marital harmony and family stability.

However, it is important to note that the Quranic directive mentioned above addresses cases where women display blatant disobedience to their husbands or fail to cooperate to maintain a recognized and harmonious marital relationship (**Ma'ruf**).

The Holy Qur'an provides men with three steps to address the behavior of disobedient women. These steps are to be followed in the order the verse prescribes: "And those wives from whom you fear arrogance, advise them, forsake them in bed, and strike them."[68]

The first step in correcting their behavior is for the husband to engage in gentle and compassionate dialogue with his wife. **فَعِظُوهُنَّ** Through reminders of Allah ﷻ, forgiveness, and the importance of preserving their marriage, the husband aims to win his wife's heart and encourage reconciliation, thus preventing further deterioration of the situation.

If this initial step does not yield positive results and the wife remains obstinately defiant, the husband may proceed to the next step. وَٱهْجُرُوهُنَّ فِى ٱلْمَضَاجِعِ This involves abstaining from conjugal relations, sleeping separately, and refraining from a normal conversation with her in bed. It is essential to note that the phrase "**in beds**" is understood by Muslim jurists to mean staying apart within the context of the bed rather than leaving the house entirely. This strategic approach allows women to reflect on

68. Quran 4:34

their behavior and understand the displeasure of their husbands, potentially leading to remorse for their actions.

Finally, if the previous steps fail to change the wife's behavior positively, the Quran suggests resorting to discipline **وَٱضۡرِبُوهُنَّۖ.** However, it should be emphasized that this discipline should never involve violence. Based on the biographical works and prophetic traditions, it is well-documented that the Prophet Muhammad ﷺ never physically harmed women or servants, even lightly. The term "**hitting**" or "**striking**" should be understood in a non-violent and gentle manner.

It is crucial to explore the context and explanations scholars provide to grasp the intended meaning of this advice. Early commentators have clarified that any physical contact should be light enough not to leave a mark (**ghayr mubarraḥ**) and done using a small object like a tooth-stick while avoiding striking the face.

This comprehensive understanding of the verse emphasizes the importance of addressing marital issues with wisdom, compassion, and respect, promoting a harmonious and balanced relationship between spouses.

4.1 Understanding "beating" or "striking" women (from the perspective of the quran and quranic commentators):

In Islam, it is evident to those who possess knowledge that the interpretation of Quranic texts is made in conjunction with the Sunnah, which refers to the traditions and practices of the Prophet Muhammad ﷺ. The understanding and implementation of the Quranic teachings were transmitted through the generations of early Muslims, mainly the companions of the Prophet and their immediate students who received authentic knowledge from them. Their profound insights and interpretations and the works of esteemed Muslim scholars throughout history, both classical and contemporary, contribute significantly to our understanding of the Quran and its sciences.

Considering this, exploring the perspectives and enlightenments these scholars offer regarding the disciplinary action mentioned in the Quranic verse concerning internal conflict resolution within marriage is valuable. Notably, the Prophet Muhammad ﷺ, being the recipient of the Quranic revelation from Allah, provided the initial interpretation of this verse. His understanding and explanation carry significant weight in shaping our comprehension of its intended meaning.

According to a narration on the authority of Amr bin Al-ahwaz AL-jashami, the prophet, ﷺ enlightened what the verse means by saying:

« استوصوا بالنساء خيرًا ، فإنهن عند كم عوان ليس تملكون منهن شيئًا غير ذلك إلا أن يأتين بفاحشة مبينة ، فإن فعلن فاهجروهن في المضاجع واضربوهن ضربًا غير مُبَرِّح ، فإن أطعنكم فلا تبغوا عليهن سبيلًا »

"Fear Allah regarding women, for they are your assistants. You have the right on them that they do not allow any person whom you dislike to step on your mat. However, if they do that, you are allowed to discipline them lightly. They have a right to you that you provide them with their provision and clothes in a reasonable manner".[69]

Based on the narration that elucidates the meaning of "وَاضْرِبُوهُنَّ" and how the beating referred to in verse should be understood, it is unanimously agreed upon by scholars that the striking mentioned in verse is to be done "**without severity**" (**ghayru mubarriḥ**) or "without causing pain" (**ghayru mu'allim**). This consensus among scholars is crucial because, without the Prophet's ﷺ, clarification, there would be a risk of husbands misusing this verse to harm women, as is unfortunately witnessed in some cases of domestic violence today, where reports of such incidents continue to rise. Here are some quotes from scholars regarding their comments on this verse, taking into account the narration mentioned earlier:

In the interpretation of this verse, various scholars have provided their insights, shedding light on the meaning of "وَاضْرِبُوهُنَّ" and how it should be understood. Here are some notable quotes from renowned scholars:

In his Tafsir, **Ibn Abbas** mentions that striking should be done in a "mild unexaggerated manner."[70]

Al-Zamakhshari states that scholars agree that the striking mentioned in the verse should be "without severity." It should not cause injury or break bones; the face should be avoided.[71]

Al-Qurtubi comments that the striking referred to in the verse

69. Al-tirmizi 1163, Al-nasa'I of Al-kubra 9169, and Ibnu Majah 1851.
70. Abbas, Ibn. 2008. *Tafsir Ibn Abbas.* Translated by Mokrane Guezzou. Louisville: Fons Vitae
71. Al-Kashshāf 4:34

"is a form of discipline without severity, aiming to rectify behavior rather than causing harm."[72]

Al-Razi mentions that "striking should be done with a folded handkerchief or the palm of the hand, emphasizing that whips or clubs should not be used."[73]

Ibn Kathir elaborates on the verse by stating, "If advice and ignoring her in the bed do not yield the desired results, one is allowed to discipline the wife without severe beating ."[74]

Ibn Hajar writes that "striking women is not allowed without restrictions, and there are situations where it is disliked or even prohibited."[75]

Al-Suyuti emphasizes that "among the rights of women is the importance of good living conditions and avoiding harm."[76]

These perspectives highlight scholars' understanding regarding the verse and provide guidance on the proper interpretation and application of the instruction within the context of marital relationships.

According to **Sayed Qutub** in his Tafsir Fii Zilal Al-Quran, the measures mentioned in the Quranic verse are intended to be pre-emptive actions aimed at achieving early reconciliation when there is a fear of rebellion. These measures should not be used to

72. Tafsīr al-Qurṭubī 4:34
73. Tafsīr al-Rāzī 4:34
74. Tafseer ibn Katheer: vol:1 page: 504.
75. Fat-hul bari vol:9 pages 302-303
76. Tafsīr al-Jalalayn 2:228.

worsen the situation or increase animosity. It is important to note that these measures are not applicable in a healthy relationship between a husband and wife. Instead, they are preventive measures to protect the family from collapsing in an unhealthy situation.[77]

Abu Al-a'la Al-Maududi also states in his work "The Meaning of the Quran" that while these measures have been permitted, they should be applied with a sense of proportion, taking into account the nature and extent of the offense. If a gentle admonition is sufficient to bring about a positive change, there is no need to resort to more severe measures. Furthermore, it is important to note that the act of beating was reluctantly allowed by the Holy Prophet and was not something that he preferred".[78]

In the translations by **Yusuf Ali**, **Wahiduddin Khan**, and **Dr. Mustapha Khattab**, the word "lightly" is added after the phrase "strike them," which signifies a necessary restriction for a correct understanding of the verse. Other commentators such as T.B. Irving, Syed Vickar Ahamed, and Dr. Munir Munshey include words like "finally," "lastly," or "if it is useful" in their interpretations. Including these additional words in English translations highlights their consensus and significance in comprehending even the fundamental meaning of the verse. This analysis provides insights into interpreting the so-called.[79]

77. Qutb, Sayyid. n.d. *In the Shade of the Quran.* Translated by Adil Salahi. Vol. 4. Kalamullah.com

78. Maududi, Abul A'la. 1976. *The Meaning of the Quran Vol II.* Lahore: Islamic Publications LTD.

79. "wife-beating verse" (4:34) of the Holy Quran, as discussed in an article published on TMV on January 20, 2019.

While some Muslim scholars vigorously defend the practice of disciplinary measures mentioned in the Quran as a divine law that is not open to discussion, they also emphasize the importance of implementing these measures in a controlled manner that avoids violence and harm to women. It is important to understand that the concept of "striking" in this context is primarily intended as a symbolic means to convey the gravity of unwarranted behavior, with divorce being the final step thereafter. The Prophet Muhammad ﷺ used similar symbolic gestures with his male companions to capture their attention and convey important messages.[80]

Regarding the application of these measures, it is crucial to ensure a proportionate response to the offense committed. It is worth mentioning that these measures should not be employed all at once but rather in cases where a wife persists in obstinate defiance. Additionally, it is evident that when a gentle approach can be effective, resorting to harsher measures should be avoided.[81]

In conclusion, from an Islamic perspective, it is prohibited to cause harm or physical injury to women through acts of violence. Under no circumstances is a husband allowed to cause bruises, injuries, or any form of harm to his wife. If a woman feels that her husband is exceeding his bounds or if she experiences physical harm, she has the legal right to seek assistance from her guardian and pursue legal action, which may include **divorce**, **khul'** (divorce upon a settlement), or **faskh** (marriage annulment). [82]

80. Abu Amina Elias, Does the Quran let men beat their wive? March 14, 2013.
81. Tafheemul Quran commentary on verse 4:35.
82. The article "Marital Harmony and Conflict Resolution: The Quranic Paradigm" by Muhammad Ziyad Batha. It was published on August 19, 2022.

The verse concludes by emphasizing that if the wives rectify themselves through the disciplinary steps mentioned, they should not be subjected to unjust treatment and should be treated with kindness and fairness (maʿrūf). This verse serves as a reminder that the ultimate solution for any dispute, including marital discord, lies in turning to Allah ﷻ.

Couples should collectively seek Allah's guidance and submit to His commands when resolving their issues and finding harmony in their relationship. By returning to Allah and following His guidance, couples can find the path to reconciliation and a peaceful resolution.

4.2 Striking or hitting women in the view of judaism:

In order to gain a comprehensive understanding of the topic and its broader dimensions, it is vital to consider the teachings of other scriptures, such as Judaism and Christianity, alongside Islam and its divine law. By conducting a comparative study, we can ensure fairness and a more nuanced perspective on the practice of disciplining wives when they display defiance. Exploring the teachings of different faiths will provide valuable insights and contribute to a well-rounded examination of this issue. **In Judaism**, it reads as follows: "A wife who refuses to perform any kind of work that she is obligated to do may be compelled to perform it, even by scourging her with a rod"[83] Also, in Deuteronomy Chapter 25 of the Bible, we read: "If two men are fighting and the wife of one of them comes to rescue her husband from his assailant, and she reaches out and seizes him by his private parts, you shall cut off her

83. Isshu 21:10

hand. Show her no pity."[84]

"What is noteworthy about this Biblical passage is that it gives the husband the authority to chop off his wife's hand. The plain reading of the verse indicates that no authorities need to get involved. The husband does not have to call the police or go before a judge. Nope, no need for any due process or any formality. He has the authority to chop up his wife himself.

Furthermore, add salt to the wound. The Bible says, Do not even show her pity,"[85]

4.3 STRIKING OR HITTING WOMEN IN THE VIEW OF CHRISTIANITY

In Christianity: From the Christian perspective, a husband's authority includes that he is entitled to have the right to discipline his wife physically. For example, Gratian's twelfth-century canon law text Decretum was highly influential in forming the Christian doctrine on spousal discipline for generations: "A man may chastise his wife and beat her for her own correction; for she is of his household, and therefore the lord may chastise his own [...] so likewise the husband is bound to chastise his wife in moderation [...] unless he be a clerk, in which case he may chastise her more severely."[86]

The Church authority Cherubino of Siena, in 1477, wrote his famous text "Rules of Married Life." In this text, he states:

---

84. Deuteronomy 25:11

85. Comparing "wife-beating" in Judaism, Christianity, Hinduism, Buddhism, and Islam: Muslim skeptic, August 7, 2022

86. (As cited in Coulton 1II.234

"When you see your wife commit an offense, do not rush at her with insults and violent blows...Scold her sharply, bully, and terrify her. And if this still does not work...take up a stick and beat her soundly, for it is better to punish the body and correct the soul than to damage the soul and spare the body...then readily beat her, not in rage but out of charity and concern for her soul, so that the beating will redound to your merit and her good."[87]

87. The Oxford Handbook of Women and Gender in Medieval Europe (New York: Oxford University Press, 2013):161-180

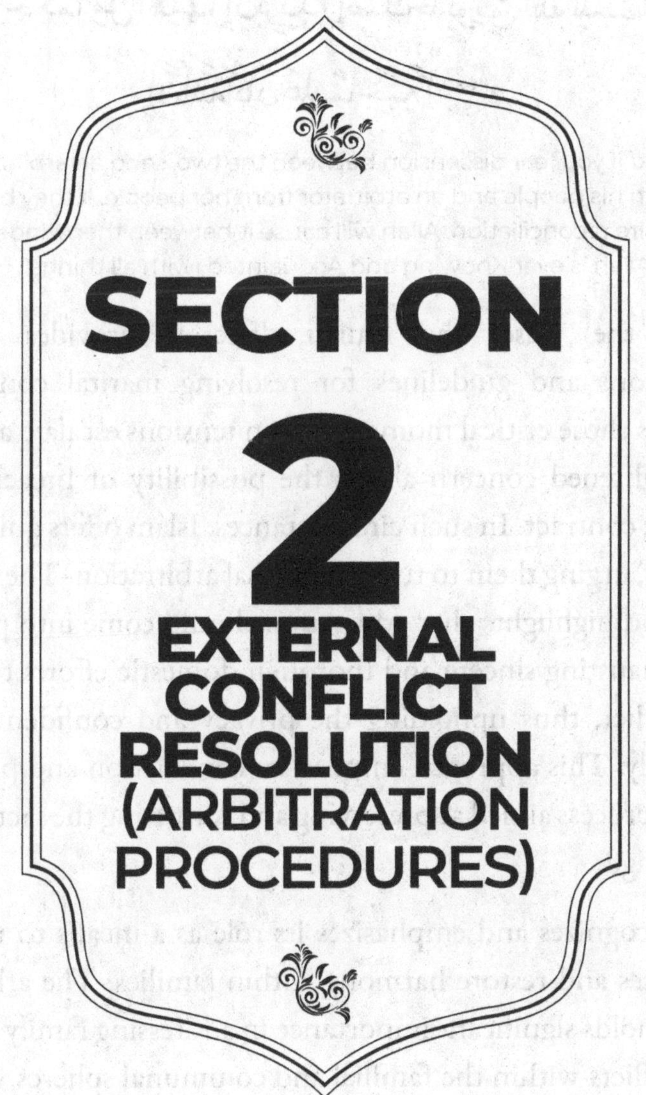

SECTION 2
EXTERNAL CONFLICT RESOLUTION (ARBITRATION PROCEDURES)

وَإِنْ خِفْتُمْ شِقَاقَ بَيْنِهِمَا فَٱبْعَثُوا۟ حَكَمًا مِّنْ أَهْلِهِۦ
وَحَكَمًا مِّنْ أَهْلِهَآ إِن يُرِيدَآ إِصْلَـٰحًا يُوَفِّقِ ٱللَّهُ بَيْنَهُمَآ ۗ
إِنَّ ٱللَّهَ كَانَ عَلِيمًا خَبِيرًا ﴿٣٥﴾

"And if you fear dissension between the two, send an arbitrator from his people and an arbitrator from her people. If they both desire reconciliation, Allah will cause it between them. Indeed, Allah is ever Knowing and Acquainted [with all things". [88]

Within the verse, the fourth directive provides ongoing instructions and guidelines for resolving marital conflicts. It addresses those critical moments when tensions escalate and there is a heightened concern about the possibility of breaching the marriage contract. In such circumstances, Islam offers guidance to believers, urging them to turn to spousal arbitration. The Quranic command highlights that arbitration should come into play only after exhausting sincere and thorough domestic efforts to resolve the conflict, thus upholding the privacy and confidentiality of the family. This approach emphasizes conciliation and presents a fruitful process aimed at preserving and nurturing the sacred bond of marriage.

Islam recognizes and emphasizes its role as a means to reconcile differences and restore harmony within families. The arbitration process holds significant importance in addressing family disputes and conflicts within the familial and communal spheres. It allows for a more expedient, wholehearted, and flexible resolution process in a less formal setting than in a courtroom environment. Similarly,

88. An-Nisa', Ayah 35

family arbitration offers a swift and efficient mechanism for couples navigating through challenging circumstances to resolve their disputes.

The arbitration procedure plays a crucial function in family disputes and conflicts on the familial and communal levels. Islam recognizes and emphasizes it as a tool to reconcile disputes and reunite families. Likewise, family arbitration is a quick process that enables couples going through family breakdowns to resolve disputes more quickly, wholeheartedly, and in a more flexible and less formal setting than a courtroom.

It is well-documented that the Arabs were familiar with and utilized arbitration to settle conflicts.

This practice was also common among other ancient civilizations and communities. Moreover, a historical examination of the Arabs and their judicial system prior to the emergence of Islam highlights the deep-rooted practice of arbitration as a means to resolve various disputes. It predates the establishment of formal state judiciary systems and even predates the formation of organized states themselves.

Furthermore, it is important to note that in the pre-Islamic era, the use of arbitration was discretionary and dependent on the voluntary agreement of the involved parties. It was primarily based on tribal customs and practices, with the chief of the tribe and respected individuals serving as arbitrators rather than relying on a formalized judicial system. This highlights the significance of arbitration as a longstanding tradition in the region, preceding the introduction of organized legal systems.[89]

Similarly to Islam, the practice of arbitration existed in pre-Islamic Arabia, where tribes would resolve disputes by referring them to a neutral third party who was trusted and respected. Islam recognized and affirmed this form of dispute resolution, indicating its compatibility with the Sharia. Historical evidence demonstrates that arbitration is not foreign to Sharia law but, on the contrary, is explicitly recommended by it. All four major schools of Islamic thought endorse arbitration with different approaches. For instance, the Hanafi school associates arbitration closely with conciliation, considering the awarded decision less binding than a court judgment.

On the other hand, the Hanbali school, known for its conservatism, considers the arbitrator's decision as binding as a court judgment, requiring the arbitrator to possess qualifications similar to a judge. This illustrates how the interpretation and application of Sharia law can vary and evolve over time, despite the fundamental principles remaining the same. This insight is found in the same source mentioned earlier.

Regarding interpreting the verse at hand, it is essential to approach it holistically rather than relying on a superficial, verse-by-verse explanatory method of tafsir. Such an atomistic approach may fail to understand the verse's depth and content comprehensively. Therefore, it is crucial to highlight the keywords of the verse in

89. "Finding your path: Arbitration, Sharia and Modern Middle East," An article published in August-September 2011.

their sequential order, as each part carries its specific meaning and is accompanied by additional rules and moral principles:

1- The Quranic enjoinment of فابعثوا
2- Nomination of the arbitrators
حكما من أهله وحكما من أهلها
3- Genuineness of the mediators
إن يريدا إصلاحا يوفق الله بينهما

1.0 THE QURANIC ENJOINMENT OF فابعثوا (SEND)

Concerning the Quranic word فابعثوا (fa'ba'thu), Muslim scholars and jurists hold different opinions regarding the addressee in the verse: Al-Tabari, in his Tafseer, suggests that the addressed person is السلطان (the ruler), and the majority of scholars widely supports this view.[90]

Al-imam Malik, representing the majority of scholars who believe the addressee is السلطان (the ruler), supports this opinion.[91]

Al-Qurtubi suggests that the addressees are the guardians of the couple.[92]

Al-imam Al-Shafie holds the opinion that the addressees are the

90. Jami'ul bayan fii ta'weel Al-Quran vol:8 pages: 318-330
91. Bidayatul Mujtahid vol: 2 page: 97, Al-Hanbila school of thought, and others
92. Vol:5, page 178

couple directly involved in the issue.[93]

Despite these differences in the scholars' views regarding the addressee, these opinions can be reconciled because each party involved has a distinct role: the ruler has the authority to command the appointment of arbitrators, and the couple has the responsibility to choose and appoint their representatives in the arbitration process since it directly concerns them. The role of the guardians may be to provide consultation to the couple and offer their opinion on the couple's choice.[94]

93. Al-Muqni Al-Muhtah vol: 2 page: 207

94. (Article: "ندب الحكمين في الخلع" "Empowering the arbitrators in the khula (divorce upon a settlement)" by Dr. Sami Abduslam, 10/6/2015, published on Aluka net.)

2.0 NOMINATION OF THE ARBITRATORS

Regarding the competence and selection of arbitrators, Ibn Kathir provides the following explanation: "The jurists have stated that in cases of disagreement between spouses, a judge appoints a reliable person from the wife's family and a trustworthy person from the husband's family to mediate and examine their situation. These individuals assess the dispute and determine whether the couple should separate or remain together to prevent further wrongdoing."[95]

The Qur'an uses the term "hakam" to refer to these appointed individuals, emphasizing their necessary qualifications. They should be capable of making a fair decision regarding the dispute, typically found in knowledgeable and trustworthy individuals. Al-Qurtubi says: "If there is a fear of dispute between spouses, it is recommended to appoint an arbitrator from the man's family and

95. Tafsir Ibn Kathir, Vol. 2, p. 447 or The Electronic copy page 1033

an arbitrator from the woman's family. These arbitrators should possess qualities of justice and a deep understanding of Islamic jurisprudence, as they are more familiar with the situation of the couple involved. If suitable candidates cannot be found among their families, then two just and knowledgeable individuals from outside can be appointed."[96]

According to Al-Qurtubi, the qualifications of the arbitrators include being just and having a comprehensive understanding of Islamic jurisprudence. Their competence is essential for successfully resolving the dispute and the goal of reuniting and fostering peace and harmony between the married couple. The requirement for arbitrators to be "Just" ensures fair treatment of both parties and encourages the conflicting couple to reconcile their differences.

96. Al-Qurtubi, Vol. 5, page 175

3.0 THE GENUINENESS OF THE MEDIATORS

"If they both desire reconciliation,
Allah will cause it between them."

According to the Quran's recommendation, "Sulh agreement" or mediation is an effective method for resolving marital disputes. It serves as an act of worship and empowers both parties, particularly the wife, to determine what is in their best interest. This process is conducted under strict confidentiality, allowing the couple to prioritize finding a mutually beneficial resolution. The Quran emphasizes the importance of the "Sulh agreement" in the chapter of Al-Nisa, encouraging couples to prioritize reconciliation and peaceful resolution." The verse reads:

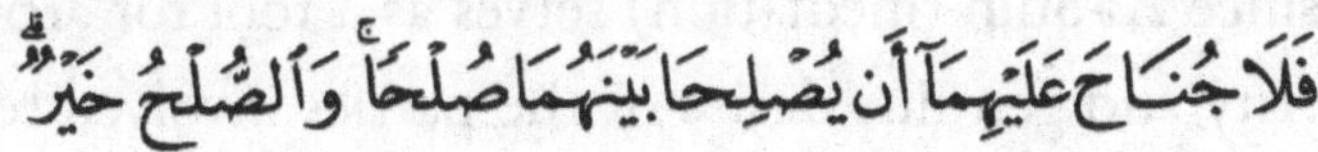

"There is no sin upon them if they make terms of settlement between them - and settlement is best." [97]

97. Al-Nisa 128

3.1 The difference between sulh agreement and arbitration:

"In Islam, arbitration differs from Sulh in three ways:

Firstly, Sulh allows for a voluntary settlement between the parties, with or without the involvement of others, while arbitration requires the appointment of a third party. Parties engaged in Sulh can use an arbitrator to reach an agreement. Thus, arbitration can serve as a tool within the Sulh process. **Secondly**, a Sulh agreement is not legally binding unless made in front of a court, whereas arbitration, according to most jurists, is enforceable without court intervention.

Thirdly, Sulh is applicable only when a conflict has already occurred and cannot be used to address potential disputes. In contrast, arbitration can be employed to resolve both existing and potential disputes."[98]

However, the verse also includes a condition at the end that highlights an aspect of the mediation process and its mechanism, as the Quran explicitly states:

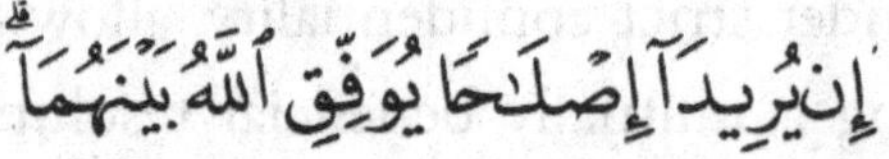

It means: "If these two arbitrators (or the couple)[99] desire to set things right, Allah Almighty will help them bring harmony between the husband and the wife."

Hence, since Al-Sulh (mediation) serves as a tool for arbitration, the sincerity and genuine desire of the parties involved to resolve

98. Aseel Al-Ramahi, Sulh: A Crucial Part of Islamic Arbitration, London School of Economics and Political Science, Law Department, p.12.
99. Al-Baqawi 8/332

the issue are crucial for the effectiveness of mediation in achieving an amicable resolution.

Regarding the insights derived from the verse regarding the arbitrators, Mohamed Shafi' Al-Othman, in his tafsir book "Maariful Quran," highlights the following:

The success of the arbitration process and the restoration of mutual rapport between the disputing couple depend on both arbitrators' good intentions and sincere desire to bring about peace. Consequently, if the desired reconciliation is not achieved, it may indicate a lack of perfect sincerity on the part of one of the arbitrators in pursuing the goal of peace-making. With the genuine efforts of the arbitrators, Allah's unseen help will facilitate the creation of love and harmony in the couple's hearts.

The appointment of the two arbitrators is specifically intended to foster peace and amity between the husband and wife without involving any other matters. However, if the parties involved in the dispute agree to appoint these arbitrators as their representatives and grant them full authority in all aspects, they would acknowledge that any decision jointly made by the arbitrators is acceptable and binding upon both of them. In such cases, the arbitrators possess absolute authority to decide the case. If they agree on divorce as the solution, it will be executed accordingly. Similarly, if they determine that the woman should be released through khul', a form of dissolution of marriage, the khul' will take effect, and their decision will be binding. Hasan al-Basri and Imam Abu Hanifah support this viewpoint.[100]

100. Ruh al-Ma'ani, etc." Al-Nisa: verse 35 - Maariful Quran: Quran.com

4.0 AUTHORITY OF THE MEDIATORS

Regarding the authority of mediators, there are differing opinions among Muslim jurists. The Hanafi and Shafi'i schools maintain that mediators typically do not possess the authority to issue a binding verdict. Their role is primarily to recommend a solution they believe is appropriate, after which the spouses have the right to accept or reject it. However, if the spouses have specifically designated the mediators to act on their behalf concerning talaq or khul' (divorce or annulment), they would be obligated to abide by the mediators' decision. This perspective is supported by the Hanafi and Shafi'i schools.

On the other hand, a group of jurists, including Hasan al-Basri and Qatadah, argue that mediators' authority is limited to facilitating reconciliation between spouses and does not extend to the annulment of the marriage.

Conversely, another group of scholars, including Ibn 'Abbas, Sa'id b. Jubayr, Ibrahim al-Nakha'i, al-Sha'bi, Muhammad b.

Sinn, and several other authorities, assert that mediators possess full authority regarding reconciliation and marriage annulment. However, Muslim jurists hold varying opinions on the extent of authority granted to mediators. While some believe mediators only provide recommendations, others argue they have the power to facilitate reconciliation and even annul marriages."[101]

In contrast to the Hanafi and Shafi'i schools, the perspective of Ibn Abbas and others emphasizes that an arbitral award holds jurisdictional significance. It is considered binding and enforceable, and the judge's role is limited to examining certain formal aspects of the arbitration process, such as a valid arbitration agreement and whether the award addresses the subject matter of the dispute. Consequently, the judge cannot refuse to enforce the arbitral decision.

It is important to note that the differences of opinion among Islamic schools of thought, as mentioned earlier, do not pertain to the authority of arbitrators to resolve the issue at hand, as they are mandated to do so by the Quran. Rather, the scholars' arguments revolve around the extent to which mediators or arbitrators can independently arrive at a final decision or issue a verdict regarding their assigned task of reconciling the couple's marital relationship or annulment.

Based on the arguments mentioned above, the prevailing juristic view asserts that arbitrators possess full authority to issue a verdict, irrespective of whether the couple accepts it. This viewpoint finds

101. Tafseer Tafheem-ul-Quran by Syed Abu-al-A'la Maududi, Al-nisa, verse 35/ Al-Mawardi: Al-hawi Al-kbeer vol:9 page 1425 / Al-Mawardi: AL-Insaf vol: 8 page 379 / I'anatu Dalibeen vol: 3:378 / Al-Kafi fii fiq Al-hanbali vol: 3 page 139.

support in the following evidence:

1- The Quran titled the arbitrators as ,حكم which means "judge. By this, the Quran endorses their authority to reach a final decision.[102]

On the authority of Ubeidah:

« ان عليا رضي الله عنه بعث رجلين فقال لهما: أتريان ما عليكما؟ عليكما إن رايتما أن تجمعا جمعتما, وإن رأيتما أن تفرقا فرقتما, فقال الرجل أما هذا فلا, فقال: كذبت والله لا تبرح حتى ترضى بكتاب الله عز وجل لك وعليك, فقالت المرأة: رضيت بكتاب الله »

> "Ali Bin Abi Talib addressed two men who appointed them as arbitrators by saying: 'Do you know your responsibility? Do you know what you must do? Hear me. If both of you agree to keep the husband and wife together and make peace between them, then do it. And if you come to the conclusion that matters cannot be set right between them or that they will not stay right later on, and both of you concur with the option that separation between them is the expedient course, then do it; the husband said: 'Separation and divorce are things I will not accept under any condition. Ali said: 'No, you are wrong. You should authorize the arbitrators; otherwise, you will depart here. When the woman heard this, she said: 'I accept the Divine law."[103]

The narration demonstrates clearly that the arbitrators have full authority and, therefore, can issue a verdict independently without referring to the judge and that the couple's acceptance is not a prerequisite in the arbitration.

102. Al-Shirazi, Al-Muhzab vol: 2 pages: 488
103. Al-Istizkar Al-jam limzahib fuqaha Al-Amsar, Hadith no: 27068 page 109.

Furthermore, a judge's intervention is only necessary when the two arbitrators differ in decision and opinion for a decisive outcome.

Finally, and far most significantly, it is worth mentioning that the only and final hope for the marital relationship's survival- if Allah wills- is the mediator's endeavor and success to save the marriage from breakdown.

Therefore, since mediation is the spouse's last chance, it is wise for the couple to show mutual respect and understanding if they wish their marriage to continue; both men and women are equally responsible and will be held countable by Allah in the hereafter should they fail to preserve the marital harmony. Hence, they are encouraged to seek help from family members or community elders, besides arbitrators, if the difficulties in their marriage seem to be developing to the worst; professional counseling might help resolve issues among couples at risk of divorcing.

4.1 Moral guidelines from verse 1 of al-talaq:

Moral values and etiquette surrounding divorce: fearing allah in the context of divorce, avoiding oppression and injustice in divorce, divorce guidelines from the Quran and Sunnah.

يَـٰٓأَيُّهَا ٱلنَّبِىُّ إِذَا طَلَّقْتُمُ ٱلنِّسَآءَ فَطَلِّقُوهُنَّ لِعِدَّتِهِنَّ وَأَحْصُوا۟
ٱلْعِدَّةَ ۖ وَٱتَّقُوا۟ ٱللَّهَ رَبَّكُمْ ۖ لَا تُخْرِجُوهُنَّ مِنۢ بُيُوتِهِنَّ
وَلَا يَخْرُجْنَ إِلَّآ أَن يَأْتِينَ بِفَـٰحِشَةٍ مُّبَيِّنَةٍ ۚ وَتِلْكَ حُدُودُ
ٱللَّهِ ۚ وَمَن يَتَعَدَّ حُدُودَ ٱللَّهِ فَقَدْ ظَلَمَ نَفْسَهُۥ ۚ لَا تَدْرِى لَعَلَّ

ٱللَّهَ يُحۡدِثُ بَعۡدَ ذَٰلِكَ أَمۡرٗا ١

"O Prophet, when you [Muslims] divorce women, divorce them for [the commencement of] their waiting period and keep count of the waiting period, and fear Allah, your Lord. Do not turn them out of their [husbands'] houses, nor should they [themselves] leave [during that period] unless they are committing a clear immorality. And those are the limits [set.

By] Allah. And whoever transgresses the limits of Allah has certainly wronged himself. You know not; perhaps Allah will bring about after that a [different] matter." [104]

The verse above emphasizes the importance of believers ending the marriage bond and parting ways amicably in situations where the mediation procedure fails or all attempts to reconcile the couple prove unsuccessful. It highlights that divorce should be seen as a last resort, a right that can be exercised when there is harm or when the couple genuinely believes they can no longer continue their relationship together.

"Sometimes divorce is obligatory when any one of the spouses causes any harm that will not be removed except with divorce. Sometimes divorce is unlawful when any one of the spouses has caused any harm, and the divorce will not bring any benefit to overcome the harm, or both the harm and the benefit are equal".[105]

From a juristic standpoint emphasizing " balancing advantages and disadvantages," divorce is considered a context-specific matter. Its permissibility or prohibition varies depending on the circumstances that arise, as illustrated in the following two narrations:

104. At-Talaq, Ayah 1
105. Minhaj al-Muslim vol:2 page 355.

A- It was narrated from ‘Abdullah bin ‘Umar that: the Messenger of Allah ﷺ said:

« عَنْ عَبْدِ اللَّهِ بْنِ عُمَر رضي الله عنه، قَالَ قَالَ رَسُولُ اللَّهِ ـ صلى الله عليه وسلم. « أَبْغَضُ الْحَلاَلِ إِلَى اللَّهِ الطَّلاَقُ » »

"The most hated of permissible things to Allah is divorce."[106]

B- It was narrated from Thawban that the Messenger of Allah, ﷺ said:

« عن ثوبان رضي الله عنه قَالَ قَالَ رَسُولُ اللَّهِ ـ صلى الله عليه وسلم أيما إمرأة سألت زوجها الطلاق في غير ما بأس فحرام عليها رائحة الجنة »

«Any woman who asks her husband for a divorce when it is not necessary, the fragrance of Paradise will be forbidden to her. »[107]

Based on the two sayings mentioned above, the first one, narrated by Abdullahi Bin Omer, highlights that divorce is something Allah ﷻ dislikes, indicating general disapproval. On the other hand, the second Hadith, narrated by Thawban, specifies that divorce is permissible when genuine harm is present in the marriage.

– **Fearing allah ﷻ:**

All the verses in the Qur’an that address marital family issues, including marriage and divorce, highlight the moral and psychological dimensions inherent in these relationships in various forms. A noticeable aspect for the reader is the consistent emphasis on the knowledge of Allah, specifically His all-knowing

106. Ibn Majah: 2018.
107. Ibid 2055

and fully encompassing of what is concealed within the depths of human beings. This notion is evident when reflecting on the concluding statements of just five verses from Surah Al-Baqara, which specifically discuss the topic of divorce. These verses (231 to 235 of Chapter Al-Baqara) are compelling examples that reinforce this observation.

1-

وَٱعْلَمُوٓا۟ أَنَّ ٱللَّهَ بِكُلِّ شَىْءٍ عَلِيمٌ ﴿٢٣١﴾

" And be mindful of Allah And know that He has full knowledge of everything." [108]

2-

وَٱللَّهُ يَعْلَمُ وَأَنتُمْ لَا تَعْلَمُونَ ﴿٢٣٢﴾

"Allah Knows, and you do not." [109]

3-

وَٱعْلَمُوٓا۟ أَنَّ ٱللَّهَ بِمَا تَعْمَلُونَ بَصِيرٌ ﴿٢٣٣﴾

"And know that Allah sees everything you do." [110]

4-

وَٱللَّهُ بِمَا تَعْمَلُونَ خَبِيرٌ ﴿٢٣٤﴾

"Allah is fully aware of what you do" [111]

5-

وَٱعْلَمُوٓا۟ أَنَّ ٱللَّهَ غَفُورٌ حَلِيمٌ ﴿٢٣٥﴾

"Remember that Allah is most forgiving and forbearing." [112]

108. Al-Baqra 231
109. Al-Baqra 232
110. Al-Baqra 233
111. Al-Baqra 234
112. Al-Baqra 235

These verses encompass the profound psychological dimensions that greatly influence the intimate aspect of the marital relationship. They serve as a reminder and warning against any injustice within this hidden realm. These dimensions are intricately defined by the innate conscience of individuals, with their nature known only to Allah the Almighty.

Similarly, the Quran emphasizes the paramount importance of Taqwa (God-consciousness) for believers. The term "Taqwa" itself is mentioned in over 60 locations throughout the Quran, while its derivatives are found in more than 190 locations across various chapters. The quality of Taqwa acts as a protective barrier, preventing the oppression of others. In the context of divorce, three specific verses emphasize the significance of Taqwa, cautioning Muslims against mistreating their wives during and after the emotionally challenging divorce process. The repetition of Taqwa in relation to divorce serves as a vital reminder for believers to stay connected with their Creator, remaining conscious of their actions and responsibilities, particularly during heated divorce moments. The three verses of "Taqwa" in surat al-talaq are:

وَمَن يَتَّقِ ٱللَّهَ يَجْعَل لَّهُۥ مَخْرَجًا ﴿٢﴾

"And whoever fears Allah - He will make for him a way out" [113]

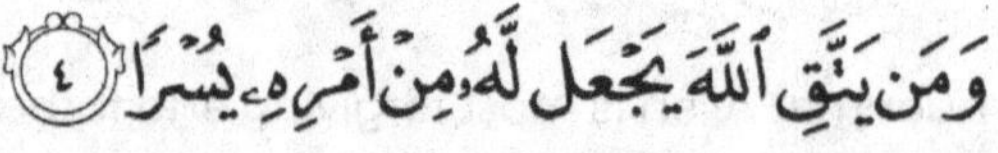

"And whoever fears Allah - He will make for him of his matter ease." [114]

113. At-Talaq, Ayah 2
114. At-Talaq, Ayah 4

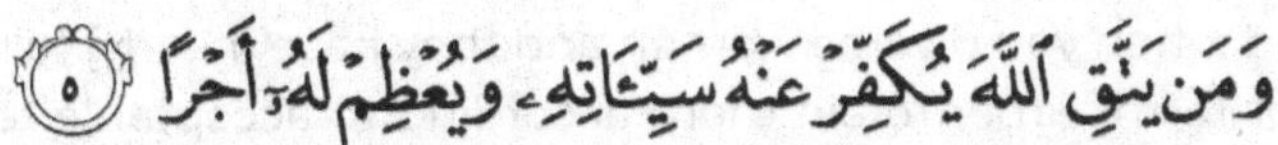

"And whoever fears Allah - He will remove for him his misdeeds and make great for him his reward." [115]

4.2 Avoiding oppression and injustice:

In a narration preserved by Imam Muslim, as mentioned previously, the Prophet Muhammad ﷺ advised, "Fear Allah in your treatment of women, for you have taken them as a trust from Allah." This profound statement highlights that oppressing and treating wives unjustly goes against Allah's trust in husbands.

Furthermore, the subsequent verses directly address the subject of divorce and clearly warn against any kind of oppression towards women. These verses emphasize that such oppression is unacceptable, regardless of the reasons or circumstances surrounding the divorce. It reinforces the importance of treating women with fairness, respect, and kindness throughout the marital relationship and during the process of divorce.

4.3 Moral teachings from verse 231 of surat al-baqrah:

وَإِذَا طَلَّقۡتُمُ ٱلنِّسَآءَ فَبَلَغۡنَ أَجَلَهُنَّ فَأَمۡسِكُوهُنَّ بِمَعۡرُوفٍ أَوۡ
سَرِّحُوهُنَّ بِمَعۡرُوفٖۚ وَلَا تُمۡسِكُوهُنَّ ضِرَارٗا لِّتَعۡتَدُواْۚ وَمَن يَفۡعَلۡ
ذَٰلِكَ فَقَدۡ ظَلَمَ نَفۡسَهُۥۚ وَلَا تَتَّخِذُوٓاْ ءَايَٰتِ ٱللَّهِ هُزُوٗاۚ وَٱذۡكُرُواْ
نِعۡمَتَ ٱللَّهِ عَلَيۡكُمۡ وَمَآ أَنزَلَ عَلَيۡكُم مِّنَ ٱلۡكِتَٰبِ وَٱلۡحِكۡمَةِ
يَعِظُكُم بِهِۦۚ وَٱتَّقُواْ ٱللَّهَ وَٱعۡلَمُوٓاْ أَنَّ ٱللَّهَ بِكُلِّ شَيۡءٍ عَلِيمٞ ٢٣١

115. At-Talaq, Ayah 5

"And when you divorce women and they have [nearly] fulfilled their term, either retain them according to acceptable terms or release them according to acceptable terms, and do not keep them, intending harm, to transgress [against them]. And whoever does that has certainly wronged himself. And do not take the verses of Allah in jest. And remember the favor of Allah upon you and what has been revealed to you of the Book and wisdom by which He instructs you. And fear Allah and know that Allah is Knowing of all things. [116]

In the mentioned verse:

- Husbands are advised against keeping their wives in a state of transgression if they no longer desire to maintain the marital relationship.
- Engaging in such oppressive behavior towards wives is regarded as a mockery of Allah's teachings and a blatant violation of their rights.

4.4 Moral teachings from verse 232 of al-baqra:

وَإِذَا طَلَّقْتُمُ ٱلنِّسَآءَ فَبَلَغْنَ أَجَلَهُنَّ فَلَا تَعْضُلُوهُنَّ أَن يَنكِحْنَ
أَزْوَٰجَهُنَّ إِذَا تَرَٰضَوْا۟ بَيْنَهُم بِٱلْمَعْرُوفِ ۗ ذَٰلِكَ يُوعَظُ بِهِۦ مَن كَانَ
مِنكُمْ يُؤْمِنُ بِٱللَّهِ وَٱلْيَوْمِ ٱلْـَٔاخِرِ ۗ ذَٰلِكُمْ أَزْكَىٰ لَكُمْ وَأَطْهَرُ ۗ وَٱللَّهُ
يَعْلَمُ وَأَنتُمْ لَا تَعْلَمُونَ ﴿٢٣٢﴾

"And when you divorce women, and they have fulfilled their term, do not prevent them from remarrying their [former] husbands if they agree among themselves on an acceptable basis. That is instructed to whoever of you believes in Allah and the Last Day. That is better for you and purer, and Allah knows, and you know not". [117]

116. Al-Baqarah, Ayah 231
117. Al-Baqarah, Ayah 232

In the verse mentioned above:
The verse prohibits preventing wives from remarrying their former husbands, as it is considered an act of oppression and injustice against them. It is worth noting that scholars have clarified that the addressee in this verse is the guardian of the wife.

- By abstaining from oppressing their wives, believers showcase their sincere and strong faith in Allah and the belief in the Hereafter.

4.5 Moral teachings from verse 4 of al-nisa:

وَءَاتُواْ ٱلنِّسَآءَ صَدُقَٰتِهِنَّ نِحۡلَةٗۚ فَإِن طِبۡنَ لَكُمۡ عَن شَيۡءٖ مِّنۡهُ نَفۡسٗا فَكُلُوهُ هَنِيٓـٔٗا مَّرِيٓـٔٗا ٤

"And give the women [upon marriage] their [bridal] gifts graciously. But if they give up willingly to you anything of it, then take it in satisfaction and ease".[118]

In verse above:
Another form of oppression is depriving wives of their rightful dowries and bridal gifts.

4.6 Moral teachings from verse 19 of al-nisa:

يَٰٓأَيُّهَا ٱلَّذِينَ ءَامَنُواْ لَا يَحِلُّ لَكُمۡ أَن تَرِثُواْ ٱلنِّسَآءَ كَرۡهٗاۖ
وَلَا تَعۡضُلُوهُنَّ لِتَذۡهَبُواْ بِبَعۡضِ مَآ ءَاتَيۡتُمُوهُنَّ إِلَّآ أَن يَأۡتِينَ
بِفَٰحِشَةٖ مُّبَيِّنَةٖۚ وَعَاشِرُوهُنَّ بِٱلۡمَعۡرُوفِۚ فَإِن كَرِهۡتُمُوهُنَّ
فَعَسَىٰٓ أَن تَكۡرَهُواْ شَيۡـٔٗا وَيَجۡعَلَ ٱللَّهُ فِيهِ خَيۡرٗا كَثِيرٗا ١٩

118. An-Nisa', Ayah 4

> "O you who have believed, it is not lawful for you to inherit women by compulsion. And do not make difficulties for them in order to take [back] part of what you gave them unless they commit a clear immorality. And live with them in kindness. For if you dislike them - perhaps you dislike a thing and Allah makes therein much good". [119]

In the verse mentioned above:

- The verse emphasizes that women cannot be treated as inheritable property, opposing the pre-Islamic custom prevalent in the Arabian peninsula. This custom forced women to marry their deceased husband's brother or closest relative against their will.
- Husbands are encouraged to treat their wives kindly and maintain good relations with them in all situations and circumstances. This includes supporting and caring for them during difficult and happy times, as harmony between spouses is crucial for a successful marital bond.

4.7 Moral teachings from verse 1 of al-talaq:

يَٰٓأَيُّهَا ٱلنَّبِيُّ إِذَا طَلَّقْتُمُ ٱلنِّسَآءَ فَطَلِّقُوهُنَّ لِعِدَّتِهِنَّ وَأَحْصُوا۟
ٱلْعِدَّةَ ۖ وَٱتَّقُوا۟ ٱللَّهَ رَبَّكُمْ ۖ لَا تُخْرِجُوهُنَّ مِنۢ بُيُوتِهِنَّ
وَلَا يَخْرُجْنَ إِلَّآ أَن يَأْتِينَ بِفَٰحِشَةٍ مُّبَيِّنَةٍ ۚ وَتِلْكَ حُدُودُ
ٱللَّهِ ۚ وَمَن يَتَعَدَّ حُدُودَ ٱللَّهِ فَقَدْ ظَلَمَ نَفْسَهُۥ ۚ لَا تَدْرِى
لَعَلَّ ٱللَّهَ يُحْدِثُ بَعْدَ ذَٰلِكَ أَمْرًا ١

119. An-Nisa', Ayah 19

> "O Prophet, when you [Muslims] divorce women, divorce them for [the commencement of] their waiting period and keep count of the waiting period, and fear Allah, your Lord. Do not turn them out of their [husbands'] houses, nor should they [themselves] leave [during that period] unless they are committing a clear immorality. And those are the limits [set by] Allah. And whoever transgresses the limits of Allah has certainly wronged himself. You know not; perhaps Allah will bring about after that a [different] matter". [120]

In verse above:

- Divorce should be conducted in accordance with the teachings of the Sunnah, which will be further discussed in subsequent pages of this section.
- It is important to note that divorced women should not be forcefully expelled from their homes until the completion of their prescribed waiting period, known as Iddah, which serves as a time of transition and reflection before considering marriage again.

وَتِلْكَ حُدُودُ ٱللَّهِ ۚ وَمَن يَتَعَدَّ حُدُودَ ٱللَّهِ فَقَدْ ظَلَمَ نَفْسَهُۥ ۚ
لَا تَدْرِى لَعَلَّ ٱللَّهَ يُحْدِثُ بَعْدَ ذَٰلِكَ أَمْرًا ﴿١﴾

(..And those are the limits [set by] Allah. And whoever transgresses the limits of Allah has certainly wronged himself) [121]

«The phrase حُدُودَ اللَّهِ (the limits prescribed by Allah) refers to the sacred laws set down by the Shari'ah of Islam. The phrase وَمَن يَتَعَدَّ (And whoever exceeds the limits prescribed by Allah) implies

120. At-Talaq, Ayah 1
121. At-Talaq 1

'whoever violates the sacred laws.' The phrase فَقَدْ ظَلَمَ نَفْسَهُ (wrongs his own self) implies that he has not damaged Allah s sacred laws or the Shari' ah. In fact, he has caused loss to himself. The loss could be religious, or it could be mundane».[122]

122. Ma'ruf Quran: Quran.com

5.0 DIVORCE GUIDELINES FROM THE QURAN AND SUNNAH

5.1 Guidelines for divorce procedures ("iddah and its rulings")

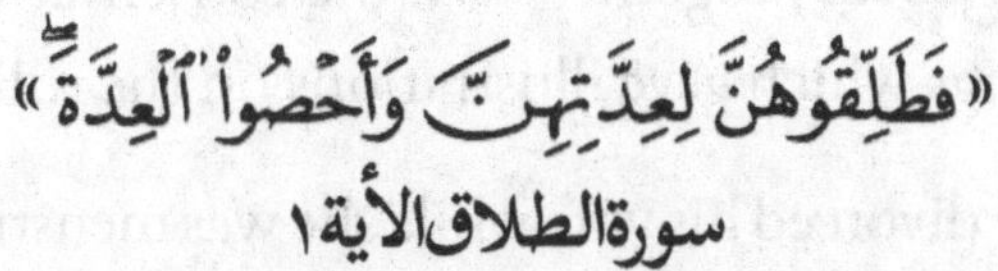

«فَطَلِّقُوهُنَّ لِعِدَّتِهِنَّ وَأَحْصُوا۟ ٱلْعِدَّةَ»

سورة الطلاق الأية ١

«Divorce them for [the commencement of] their waiting period and keep count of the waiting period. » 123

In this verse, divorce categorization and guidelines according to Quran and Sunnah:

Category 1: Sunni Divorce (الطلاق السني) - This refers to a divorce pronounced during the wife's state of purity, wherein the husband has not engaged in any sexual intercourse with her. In such cases, the husband must wait until the wife's next state of

123. Al-Talaq 1

purity after menstruation before proceeding with the divorce.

Category 2: Innovated Divorce (الطلاق البدعي) - This refers to a divorce pronounced by the husband in certain prohibited situations, which include:

a- During the wife's menstruation period.
b- During the wife's postnatal period.
c- During the wife's state of purity after engaging in sexual intercourse.
d- Pronouncing divorce thrice in one word or repeating it three times simultaneously, such as saying, "She is divorced, she is divorced, she is divorced."[124]

However, the above rulings and restrictions concerning divorce, its way, and time can be provable through the prophetic traditions that elaborate the meaning of the Quranic commandment (فَطَلِّقُوهُنَّ لِعِدَّتِهِنَّ وَأَحْصُوا۟ ٱلْعِدَّةَ) together with the consensus of the scholars and their sayings which gave illustrations on the rulings involved:

– Ibn 'Umar divorced his wife while she was menstruating. When 'Umar ibnulkhatab mentioned this to the Messenger of Allah, ﷺ heard this, he became very indignant and said:

« مره ليراجعها ثم يمسكها حتّى تطهر ثم تحيض فتطهر ،
فان بدا له فليطلقها طاهرًاقبل ان يمسّها ، فتلك العدّه الّتى

124. Wahbat Zuheili, Al-fiqh Al-shafi'i Al-Muyasar, Vol. 2, pages 124-127. Abu al-Hassan, Bidayat al-Mubtadi, p. 68. Tha'labi, al-Talqeen fi al-Fiqh al-Maliki, Vol. 1, p. 124-125. Nawawi, Rawdat al-Talibeen, Vol. 8, p. 3-8. Minhajul Muslim, Vol. 2, page 358.

امرها اللہ تعالیٰ ان یطلّق بها النّساء۔ »

"He must take her back and keep her till she is purified, then has another menstrual cycle and is purified. If it then seems proper for him to pronounce another divorce to her, he may do so when she is pure from the menstrual discharge before having conjugal relations with her, for that is the 'iddah that Allah has commanded for the divorce of women."[125]

- Al-imam Bukhari commented on the narration by saying: «The Sunnah Talaq is to divorce her in a state of purity with no intercourse and in the presence of two witnesses. »[126]
- Ibnu Rushd mentioned that there is a scholarly consensus, a binding proof, on this issue whereby he said in his book of Bidyat Al-mujtahid:

« The jurists have unanimously agreed that Sunnah divorce concerning the consummated marriage is to pronounce the divorce on the wife in a state of purity in which he did not have intercourse with her and the one who divorces during the menses period, he did not divorce following the Sunnah. »[127]

Furthermore, it is important to highlight that according to Ibn Rushd's interpretation in the quotation above, the phrase "the consummated marriage" refers to a marriage that has been physically consummated through sexual intercourse. In the case of a marriage that has not been consummated yet, the husband has the right to divorce his wife at any time, regardless of her state of purity. This is because the waiting period (iddah) mentioned in the Quranic verse in Surat Al-Ahzab does not apply in such a

125. Sahih Bukhari 5251 and Muslim 1471.
126. Sahih Al-Bukhari 7/52.
127. Ibnu Rushd, Bidayat Al-Mujtahid, vol: 3 pages: 86.

situation. The ruling regarding divorce without a waiting period specifically applies to marriages that have not been consummated. The Quran says:

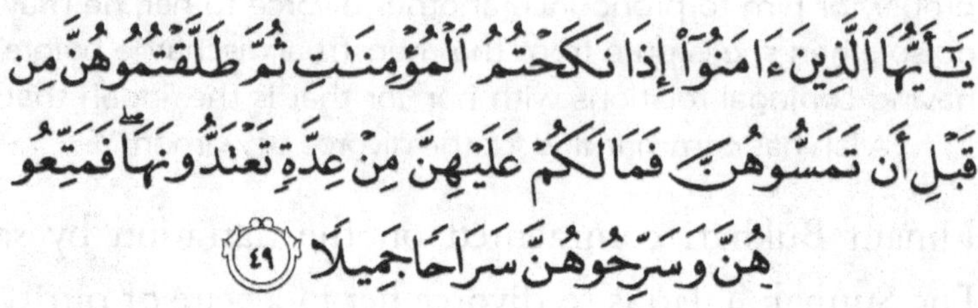

«O You who have believed, when you marry believing women and then divorce them before you have touched them, then there is not for you any waiting period to count concerning them. So, provide for them and give them a gracious release».[128]

To provide further clarification on the ruling mentioned in the Quranic verse, it states that if a woman is divorced before the consummation of her marriage, meaning before any sexual intercourse takes place with her husband, she is not subject to the waiting period (iddah) rulings mentioned earlier. Therefore, she is not required to comply with those specific rulings. On the other hand, if a woman has consummated her marriage and had sexual contact with her husband, she is obligated to observe the waiting period (iddah), during which she is expected to preserve the rights of both her husband and herself.

Furthermore, divorcing a wife by uttering the word "divorced" three times in one instance is not in accordance with the Sunnah. The Prophet expressed his disapproval when he heard that a man had divorced his wife by pronouncing three divorces in one statement without any interval between them. This incident is

128. Al-Ahzab, Ayah 49

mentioned in the following Hadith: On the authority of Mahmud Bin Labid, he said:

« اخبرني رسول الله صلى الله عليه وسلم عن رجل طلق إمرأته ثلاث تطيقات جميعا فغضب وقال : أيلعب بكتاب الله وأنا بين أظهركم ؟ »

«That, when the prophet was informed about a man who divorced his wife with three pronouncements in one word, the prophet ﷺ became angry and said: « Is play being made of Allah's book while I am among you? »[129]

However, there is a difference of opinion among scholars regarding the effectiveness of "**innovated divorce**" in breaking the marriage bond, despite it being disliked in the Sharia. The majority of scholars hold the view that innovative divorce does indeed have an impact and ultimately leads to the dissolution of the marital bond.

5.2 The wisdom behind following the sunnah in divorce; how and when

The Divine legislation surrounding the strict guidelines, stipulations, and restrictions on divorce carries within it valuable wisdom and primary goals, including the following:

The preservation of the spousal relationship is one of the main objectives of the Sharia, emphasizing the importance of maintaining strong family bonds through all available means.

Removing obstacles and barriers that may separate a husband and wife is a key consideration. Therefore, divorce should only be pronounced during the wife's state of purity, signifying the

129. Al-Nasaa'i, vol: 6, pages: 143-144.

husband's willingness to reconsider his decision and thoughts of divorce.

The verse "You know not; perhaps Allah will bring about after that a [different] matter" (At-Talaq, verse 1) indicates the potential for change during the waiting period (Iddah). It suggests that the couple may reconcile and experience a better relationship. These profound words from the Quran highlight the psychological transformation that can occur during this period, where the husband may reflect on the comforts and services provided by his wife in managing the household and caring for their children. This reflection may lead to remorse, prompting him to retract the divorce and reconcile with his wife.

The Iddah (waiting period) should not be unnecessarily prolonged. If divorce occurs during menstruation, the Iddah may start from the next menstrual cycle. Conversely, if divorce happens during purity, the Iddah may start from her immediate menstruation period. This approach ensures that the wife's waiting period is efficiently managed, saving her time.

Intercourse during the non-menstruating period, known as "tuhr," should be avoided to prevent the possibility of pregnancy. In such cases, the Iddah period will only conclude once the wife gives birth to the child. This situation may result in a more extended waiting period, similar to divorce during the menstrual period.

In summary, the Divine legislation surrounding divorce serves several significant purposes, including preserving marital bonds, the potential for reconciliation, efficient management of the Iddah period, and considerations related to pregnancy.

5.3 Iddah and its rulings:

« فَطَلِّقُوهُنَّ لِعِدَّتِهِنَّ وَأَحْصُوا۟ ٱلْعِدَّةَ » الطلاق ١

«Divorce them for [the commencement of] their waiting period and keep count of the waiting period. » [130]

And the previous narration of Bukhari[131] and Muslim[132] on the authority of Ibn Umar:

« فتلك العدّه الّتی امرها الله تعالیٰ ان یطلّق بها النّساء »

«..for that is the 'iddah that Allah has commanded for the divorce of women.»

As previously discussed, the verse mentioned above serves as the foundation for the concept of Iddah and its associated rulings. Muslim jurists and Quran commentators have further elaborated on these matters, drawing insights from explanatory prophetic traditions, including the narration of Ibn Umar mentioned earlier. These elaborations shed light on the various rulings and rights pertaining to Iddah and its procedures. The following are some of the key rulings and rights concerning Iddah:

- **Iddah and its prescribed period*:***

- **Definitions and objectives of iddah (maqasid al-iddah)**

Definition of Iddah: Iddah is an Islamic concept pertaining to divorce and a husband's death. Derived from Arabic, it signifies a legally prescribed waiting period during which a woman is not

130. Al-Talaq 1.
131. 5251
132. 1471

permitted to remarry after being widowed or divorced.

The observance of Iddah serves several primary purposes:

- Establishing pregnancy and determining the legitimate paternity of a child before allowing remarriage in cases of divorce or death.
- Allowing a period for potential reconciliation, as divorce is considered a last resort in resolving family problems according to prescribed measures.
- Providing a mourning period for the deceased husband, whose companionship is terminated by death.
- Granting a waiting period in case a husband has disappeared, allowing the woman time before considering remarriage.
- Ensuring that a woman receives the necessary care and support during pregnancy, particularly following the death of her husband.[133]

5.4 The prescribed period of iddah

There are four categories of women with specific durations of Iddah prescribed for each, as determined by Islamic teachings and supported by references from the Quran.

- The first category pertains to pregnant women, whether widowed or divorced, whose Iddah period concludes upon delivery of the child.

133. Dr. Busari Mshood, "Iddatul-talaq and iddatul wafat: A re-interpretation of the phrase 'Hatta yada'na hamlahuna'" (2017).

Allah ﷻ says:

«وَأُوْلَٰتُ ٱلْأَحْمَالِ أَجَلُهُنَّ أَن يَضَعْنَ حَمْلَهُنَّ» الطلاق ٤

«...And for those who are pregnant, their term is until they give birth» [134]

- The second category pertains to non-pregnant widows, for whom the prescribed duration of Iddah is four months and ten days following the death of their husband. The Quran states:

«وَٱلَّذِينَ يُتَوَفَّوْنَ مِنكُمْ وَيَذَرُونَ أَزْوَٰجًا يَتَرَبَّصْنَ بِأَنفُسِهِنَّ أَرْبَعَةَ أَشْهُرٍ وَعَشْرًا فَإِذَا بَلَغْنَ أَجَلَهُنَّ» ﴿٤٣٢﴾

"And those who are taken in death among you and leave wives behind - they, [the wives, shall] wait four months and ten [days]." [135]

- The third category pertains to menstruating women, for whom the prescribed duration of Iddah is three menstrual cycles. Verse in Surat Al-Baqra mentions:

«وَٱلْمُطَلَّقَٰتُ يَتَرَبَّصْنَ بِأَنفُسِهِنَّ ثَلَٰثَةَ قُرُوٓءٍ»
البقرة ﴿٨٢٢﴾

«Divorced women remain in waiting for three periods» [136]

- The fourth category pertains to women who do not menstruate due to being either too young or too old. For such women, the prescribed duration of Iddah is typically a period of three lunar

134. At-Talaq verse: 4
135. Al-Baqarah, Ayah 234
136. Al-Baqarah, Ayah 228

months. Allah says:

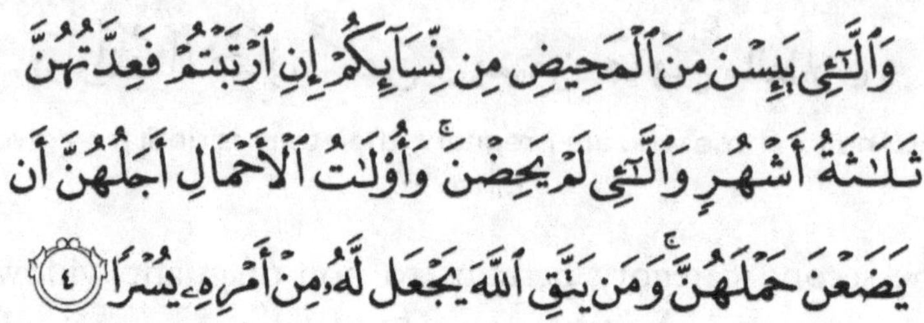

«..And those who no longer expect menstruation among your women - if you doubt, then their period is three months, and [also for] those who have not menstruated». [137]

5.5 Rights and obligations during iddah:

The divorced wife, under revocable divorce (طلاق رجعة), cannot enter into a marriage contract with another man, as the divorce is still revocable, indicating that the previous marriage is not entirely terminated.

During the revocable period of Iddah, the husband has the right to reconcile and resume the marital relationship without requiring the wife's acceptance or permission. However, in cases of irrevocable divorce, the divorcing man no longer possesses this right. Once an irrevocable divorce takes effect, he is treated like any other man seeking to marry her. She can accept him for a new marriage with a new contract and dowry if desired. Alternatively, she can reject and refuse him. Irrevocable divorce may occur when:

a- The prescribed period of Iddah concludes.
b- Divorce is initiated through Khul' (mutual separation) or arbitration.

137. At-Talaq, Ayah 4

c- Divorce occurs before the consummation of marriage (prior to sexual relations), as mentioned earlier.

d- Divorce is pronounced for the third time after completing two previous divorces.)[138]

As the wifely-related rulings continue during the Iddah period, the divorced wife has the right to receive full financial support, housing accommodation, and other necessary provisions until her prescribed period is completed.

In the event of pregnancy, she is obligated to inform her husband as it affects the extension of the Iddah period and relates to the child he will father.

138. Minhajul Muslim vol: 2 pages:359-360

SECTION 3

ETIQUETTE AND MORALITY TOWARD PARENTS

1.0 THE SIGNIFICANCE OF ETIQUETTE AND MORALITY TOWARDS PARENTS IN ISLAMIC TEACHINGS

This topic holds a unique and significant scope, focusing on the parent-child code of behavior. It encompasses various dimensions, including qualities such as forgiveness, patience, and respect toward parents. Islam, unlike any other religion, emphasizes the utmost respect and care towards parents, with no comparable level of importance given to any other relationship except that of the Prophet ﷺ. What sets this code apart is its foundation in the divine law of Allah ﷻ, which exemplifies its perfection and completeness.

Searching for "kindness to parents" on Google shows that six out of the first ten results are Islamic articles highlighting the importance of being dutiful and kind to parents. This prominence is due to Islam being a religion that emphasizes qualities such as mercy, tolerance, and respect. God has commanded the good treatment of parents and warned against treating them with disrespect.[139]

Moreover, the methodology of sublime morality regarding parent-child relations adopted by Islam surpasses that of other religions and culturally-based morals and etiquettes. The Quran's commandments and the Prophet Muhammad's teachings ﷺ contain balanced imperatives that cultivate healthy and positive relationships, encompassing mutual obligations and reciprocal arrangements on both sides.

A study of various Quranic verses concerning parents reveals the elevated status that Allah ﷻ has bestowed upon them. Islam decrees respect for parents immediately after believing in Allah and worshiping Him alone, emphasizing the tremendous value of this obligation. The Holy Qur'an underscores this obligation by mentioning it more than fifteen times, emphasizing our indebtedness to our parents and the extensive rights we owe them.

As we delve into the Quranic commandments and the sayings of the Prophet Muhammad ﷺ, it becomes evident that compassion, reverence, and respect towards parents hold exceptional importance in the Islamic way of life. The revelations regarding this theme are abundant and highlight the qualities mentioned thus far, along with others that further emphasize how deeply these moral values

139. Aisha Stacey, "Kindness to Parents: Duty and Devotion." Published on July 21, 2008, on IslamReligion.com.

are embedded in the teachings of Islam.

– THE HOLY QURAN:

Allah ﷻ says in the Holy Quran the following:

وَإِذْ أَخَذْنَا مِيثَٰقَ بَنِىٓ إِسْرَٰٓءِيلَ لَا تَعْبُدُونَ إِلَّا ٱللَّهَ وَبِٱ
لْوَٰلِدَيْنِ إِحْسَانًا وَذِى ٱلْقُرْبَىٰ وَٱلْيَتَٰمَىٰ وَٱلْمَسَٰكِينِ وَقُو
لُوا۟ لِلنَّاسِ حُسْنًا وَأَقِيمُوا۟ ٱلصَّلَوٰةَ وَءَاتُوا۟ ٱلزَّكَوٰةَ ثُمَّ
تَوَلَّيْتُمْ إِلَّا قَلِيلًا مِّنكُمْ وَأَنتُم مُّعْرِضُونَ ﴿٨٣﴾

"And [recall] when We took the covenant from the Children of Israel, [enjoining upon them], "Do not worship except Allah; and to parents do good and to relatives, orphans, and the needy. And speak to people good [words] and establish prayer and give zakah." Then you turned away, except a few of you, and you were refusing." [140]

In the Quran, Allah ﷻ consistently emphasizes the duty of being kind and compassionate to our parents in close proximity to the command to worship Him alone. This parallel placement of Allah's rights and parents' rights signifies their simultaneous importance and serves as a reminder of their intertwined significance within one verse.

– He ﷻ also says:

۞ وَٱعْبُدُوا۟ ٱللَّهَ وَلَا تُشْرِكُوا۟ بِهِۦ شَيْـًٔا ۖ وَبِٱلْوَٰلِدَيْنِ إِحْسَٰنًا وَبِذِى

140. Al-Baqarah, Ayah 83

ٱلْقُرْبَىٰ وَٱلْيَتَٰمَىٰ وَٱلْمَسَٰكِينِ وَٱلْجَارِ ذِى ٱلْقُرْبَىٰ وَٱلْجَارِ
ٱلْجُنُبِ وَٱلصَّاحِبِ بِٱلْجَنۢبِ وَٱبْنِ ٱلسَّبِيلِ وَمَا مَلَكَتْ
أَيْمَٰنُكُمْ ۗ إِنَّ ٱللَّهَ لَا يُحِبُّ مَن كَانَ مُخْتَالًا فَخُورًا ﴿٣٦﴾

"Worship Allah and associate nothing with Him, and to parents do good, and to relatives, orphans, the needy, the near neighbor, the neighbor farther away, the companion at your side, the traveler, and those whom your right hands possess. Indeed, Allah does not like those who are self-deluding and boastful". [141]

– Repeating the same injunction, Allah ﷻ says:

۞ قُلْ تَعَالَوْا۟ أَتْلُ مَا حَرَّمَ رَبُّكُمْ عَلَيْكُمْ ۖ أَلَّا تُشْرِكُوا۟
بِهِۦ شَيْـًٔا ۖ وَبِٱلْوَٰلِدَيْنِ إِحْسَٰنًا ۖ وَلَا تَقْتُلُوٓا۟ أَوْلَٰدَكُم مِّنْ
إِمْلَٰقٍ ۖ نَّحْنُ نَرْزُقُكُمْ وَإِيَّاهُمْ ۖ وَلَا تَقْرَبُوا۟ ٱلْفَوَٰحِشَ مَا
ظَهَرَ مِنْهَا وَمَا بَطَنَ ۖ وَلَا تَقْتُلُوا۟ ٱلنَّفْسَ ٱلَّتِى حَرَّمَ
ٱللَّهُ إِلَّا بِٱلْحَقِّ ۚ ذَٰلِكُمْ وَصَّىٰكُم بِهِۦ لَعَلَّكُمْ تَعْقِلُونَ ﴿١٥١﴾

"Say, "Come, I will recite what your Lord has prohibited to you. [He commands] that you not associate anything with Him, and to parents, good treatment, and do not kill your children out of poverty; We will provide for you and them. And do not approach immoralities - what is apparent of them and what is concealed. And do not kill the soul which Allah has forbidden [to be killed] except by [legal] right. This has He instructed you that you may use reason". [142]

141. An-Nisa', Ayah 36
142. Al-An'am, Ayah 15

Once again, in the preceding two verses, the focus on Tawheed, the belief in the oneness of Allah and worshiping Him alone, is evident. This emphasis is then followed by a command to display compassion towards parents and relatives, as highlighted in verse 36 of Al-Nisa, and to refrain from committing various grave sins, as mentioned in Al-An'am verse 152. These divine instructions from our Merciful Creator address the needs and obligations of both parents and children, ensuring that neither is neglected.

However, it is vital to acknowledge the psychological aspect of this matter. The younger generation naturally tends to look forward rather than backward, focusing on their own aspirations and the well-being of their own offspring. Yet, it is crucial to recognize that parents hold a significant place in our lives. They are the ones who brought us into this world and played a pivotal role in our upbringing, which significantly contributes to our eventual success and development.

By emphasizing the obligation of compassion and kindness towards parents, the verses aim to remind children of the profound debt of gratitude they owe to their parents above anyone else. It is a reminder of the immense sacrifice and effort parents have invested in raising their children. Recognizing and fulfilling this duty of compassion becomes essential for maintaining a harmonious and balanced society.

However, the verses emphasize the importance of Tawheed, worshiping Allah alone, while also highlighting the significance of displaying kindness and compassion towards parents and avoiding sinful actions. They address the innate tendency of younger individuals to focus on their own future, urging them to reflect upon the vital role parents play in their lives. Parents deserve our utmost compassion and respect as the source of our existence and instrumental figures in our upbringing.[143]

۞ وَقَضَىٰ رَبُّكَ أَلَّا تَعْبُدُوٓا۟ إِلَّآ إِيَّاهُ وَبِٱلْوَٰلِدَيْنِ إِحْسَٰنًا ۚ إِمَّا
يَبْلُغَنَّ عِندَكَ ٱلْكِبَرَ أَحَدُهُمَآ أَوْ كِلَاهُمَا فَلَا تَقُل لَّهُمَآ
أُفٍّ وَلَا تَنْهَرْهُمَا وَقُل لَّهُمَا قَوْلًا كَرِيمًا ﴿٢٣﴾
وَٱخْفِضْ لَهُمَا جَنَاحَ ٱلذُّلِّ مِنَ ٱلرَّحْمَةِ وَقُل رَّبِّ ٱرْحَمْهُمَا
كَمَا رَبَّيَانِى صَغِيرًا ﴿٢٤﴾

"And your Lord has decreed that you not worship except Him, and to parents, good treatment. Whether one or both of them reach old age [while] with you, say not to them [so much as], "uff," and do not repel them but speak to them a noble word. And lower to them the wing of humility out of mercy and say, "My Lord, have mercy upon them as they brought me up [when I was] small."[144]

This passage, encompassing two verses and a famous verse from the Quran regarding parent-child relations, effectively delves into the subject matter's profound depth and various dimensions. If there were no other verses addressing the moral behavior between parents and children, these two verses would still be sufficient to convey the comprehensive message encompassing all aspects of the discourse.

143. Fizilal Al-Quran p.123
144. Al-Isra', Ayah 23- 24.

However, the articles within these Quranic directives explicitly proclaim the rights of parents alongside the rights of Allah ﷻ, establishing the primacy of parental rights as the greatest among all human rights. Thus, these verses extend beyond mere moral recommendations; they form the foundation of parental rights and authority, with further details elucidated in the Books of Hadith and Fiqh, as eloquently expressed by Abu A'la in his book "Al-Tafheem." Furthermore, demonstrating respectful behavior, obedience, and honoring the rights of parents constitutes an indispensable element of both practical education and moral training within Islamic society and civilization, as emphasized in verses 23-27 of "Al-Tafheem."[145]

Additionally, the passage imparts a valuable practical lesson, teaching us the significance of prioritizing love, affection, kindness, and mercy towards our parents, particularly as they age and become dependent on our care. Thus, the duty to prioritize and prioritize our parents' needs and well-being over other obligations is firmly emphasized. This concept was also emphasized by the Prophet Muhammad ﷺ in one of his sayings. On a specific occasion, when directing one of his companions, he emphasized the need to prioritize serving one's parents over engaging in Al-jihad (striving for the cause of Islam) and Al-hijrah (migrating for the sake of Islam). This profound teaching, narrated by Abdullah ibn Umar, serves as a powerful reminder of the paramount importance of filial piety and caring for our parents throughout their lives, especially during their elder years.

145. verses 23-27 "Al-Tafheem.

« أقبل رجل إلى نبي الله صلى الله عليه وسلم فقال: أبايعك على»الهجرة والجهاد، أبتغي الأجر من الله، قال: »فهل من والديك أحد حي؟» قال: نعم، بل كلاهما، قال: »فتبتغي الأجر من الله؟» قال: نعم، قال: »فارجع إلى والديك فأحسن صحبتهما »

"A man came to the Prophet of Allah ﷺ and said: I pledge allegiance to you on immigration and jihad, seeking reward from God. He said: Are any of your parents alive? He said: Yes, but both of them. So he said: Do you seek reward from God? He said: Yes, he said: Go back to your parents and be good to them".[146]

The core purpose of Islamic teachings regarding the treatment of parents is to express and bestow upon them our profound mercy. Mercy is the foundational moral behavior our parents deserve, and it is the central theme emphasized in this passage. Mercy, in essence, is the compassionate sentiment that fosters a deep emotional bond between parents and their children, encompassing both material and spiritual aspects.

Furthermore, the verses within the Quran acknowledge that there may be instances when one or both parents exhibit exceedingly challenging or offensive behavior. Even in such circumstances, it is strictly forbidden to neglect or show annoyance towards our parents. Neglect and annoyance demonstrate a lack of respect and gratitude toward those who have raised and supported us throughout our lives. If it becomes necessary to address their behavior, it should be done with patience, open communication, and a sincere effort to

146. Bukhari 3004

peacefully resolve the issue. Regardless of the situation, one should refrain from expressing mild disgust or disapproval. Instead, from a young age, children should be taught to respect and honor the elderly. They should exhibit tolerance towards their parents, even during tense moments, showing restraint and refraining from speaking ill of them, especially considering any capricious behavior as a sign of old age. It is equally important to extend respect to the parents of one's spouse, as these actions further nurture love and harmony within the marital relationship.

The emphasis placed on honoring parents in Islam is so significant that Muslims consider it an exceptional opportunity to attain paradise through serving one's parents. Sadly, many individuals fail to seize this immense blessing bestowed upon them. Regrettably, only those fortunate enough to grasp this rare and precious chance can truly benefit from it. The Prophet Muhammad ﷺ warns against neglecting this reward, as it serves as a means to ultimately achieve our goal of entering paradise.

The teachings of Islam stress the significance of showing mercy to parents, which forms the bedrock of their treatment. The passage emphasizes the importance of compassionately caring for our parents and addresses navigating challenging situations with patience and respect. It also underscores the immense reward associated with fulfilling the rights of parents, highlighting the opportunity it provides to attain paradise.

On the authority of Abuhuraira, the prophet ﷺ said:

« رغم أنف ثم رغم أنف ثم رغم أنف قيل من يا رسول الله

قال من أدرك أبويه عند الكبر أحدهما أو كليهما فلم يدخل الجنة »

"May a man whose parents reached old age in his presence, and they were not a cause for his entrance to Paradise (by being dutiful to them), be humiliated."[147]

Hence, one of the most significant acts that pave the way to paradise is Birrul Walideen, which encompasses both obedience and treating parents with kindness and respect. This concept of Birrul Walideen holds tremendous importance in Islam, as it is regarded as one of the best and most beloved deeds in the sight of Allah, second only to prayer.

In a report by Ibnu mas'ud, the messenger ﷺ said:

« سألت رسول الله صلى الله عليه وسلم: »أي العمل أحب إلى الله قال: الصلاة على وقتها. قال ثم أي؟ قال: ثم بر الوالدين. قال: ثم أي؟ قال: الجهاد في سبيل الله« قال حدثني بهن ولو استزدته لزادني »

"The best of the deeds or deed is the (observance of) prayer at its proper time and kindness to the parents."[148]

Conversely, disobeying and mistreating parents can lead to the consequences of hellfire. Abu al-Faraj Ibn Al-Jawzi eloquently expands on the ethical concept of "al-birr" and how it should be manifested in our behavior and manners towards our parents. He emphasizes that being kind to our parents entails obeying their

147. Tirmidhi 3545.
148. Sahih Muslim 85

commands unless they ask us to do something forbidden by Allah, prioritizing their instructions over voluntary acts of worship, refraining from what they forbid us to do, providing for their needs, serving them, approaching them with humility and mercy, refraining from raising our voice or fixing our gaze on them, and avoiding calling them by their names. Patience in dealing with them is also essential. [149]

It is crucial to exercise caution and refrain from using insulting interjections when communicating with our parents.[150] In the Quran, Allah commands us not to even utter the smallest disrespectful comment towards our parents. Even saying "uff" to our parents is considered inappropriate.

The word **"uff"** is an interjection that expresses displeasure and should not be used when conversing with our parents.

Furthermore, the verses in the Quran guide us not to scold or reprimand our parents due to their old age. Instead, we should treat them with kindness and supplicate to Allah, asking Him to shower them with His mercy, just as they have shown us mercy during our childhood. Since Allah's blessings and favors are bestowed through His mercy, seeking Allah's mercy for our parents encompasses seeking all other divine blessings.

According to Al-Ghazali, the happiness of children in this world and the hereafter depends on the prayers of their parents. The prayers of parents are accepted and hold immense weight.

---

149. Ibn al-Jawzi, Birr al-Wâlidayn, page 5, Pdf.
150. Abu Mahdi, an article: parents in the Quran, September 22, 2020

Neglecting or upsetting our parents carries a tremendous sin, equivalent to the weight of mountains. Failing to respond to our parents' calls burdens our souls significantly (Ibid). Al-Ghazali emphasizes that those with a conscience should not bring distress to their parents, as the consequences are severe.

The Prophet Muhammad ﷺ highlighted the correlation between parental satisfaction and attaining the pleasure of Allah ﷻ. If parents are pleased with their children, it is an indication that they have also attained Allah's pleasure. Conversely, if parents are displeased with their children, it signifies a lack of Allah's pleasure ﷺ. This emphasizes the immense importance of maintaining a strong and respectful bond with our parents[151]

On the authority of Abdullah ibn Umar the Prophet ﷺ said: :

« رضى الرب في رضى الوالد , وسخط الرب في سخط الوالد»

"The Lord's pleasure is in the parent's pleasure, and the Lord's anger is in the parent's anger,"[152]

Allah ﷻ says in the following chapters of Al-ankabut, Luqman, and Al-ahqaf:

وَوَصَّيْنَا ٱلْإِنسَٰنَ بِوَٰلِدَيْهِ حُسْنًا ۖ وَإِن جَٰهَدَاكَ لِتُشْرِكَ بِى مَا لَيْسَ لَكَ بِهِۦ
عِلْمٌ فَلَا تُطِعْهُمَآ ۚ إِلَىَّ مَرْجِعُكُمْ فَأُنَبِّئُكُم بِمَا كُنتُمْ تَعْمَلُونَ ٨

"And We have enjoined upon man goodness to parents. But

151. Ibid.
152. Tirmidhi 1899

if they endeavor to make you associate with Me that of which you have no knowledge, do not obey them. To Me is your return, and I will inform you about what you used to do".[153]

وَوَصَّيْنَا ٱلْإِنسَٰنَ بِوَٰلِدَيْهِ حَمَلَتْهُ أُمُّهُۥ وَهْنًا عَلَىٰ وَهْنٍ وَفِصَٰلُهُۥ
فِى عَامَيْنِ أَنِ ٱشْكُرْ لِى وَلِوَٰلِدَيْكَ إِلَىَّ ٱلْمَصِيرُ ﴿١٤﴾

"And We have enjoined upon man [care] for his parents. His mother carried him, [increasing her] in weakness upon weakness, and his weaning is in two years. Be grateful to Me and to your parents; to Me is the [final] destination".[154]

وَوَصَّيْنَا ٱلْإِنسَٰنَ بِوَٰلِدَيْهِ إِحْسَٰنًا ۖ حَمَلَتْهُ أُمُّهُۥ كُرْهًا وَوَضَعَتْهُ
كُرْهًا ۖ وَحَمْلُهُۥ وَفِصَٰلُهُۥ ثَلَٰثُونَ شَهْرًا ۚ حَتَّىٰٓ إِذَا بَلَغَ أَشُدَّهُۥ وَبَلَغَ
أَرْبَعِينَ سَنَةً قَالَ رَبِّ أَوْزِعْنِىٓ أَنْ أَشْكُرَ نِعْمَتَكَ ٱلَّتِىٓ أَنْعَمْتَ
عَلَىَّ وَعَلَىٰ وَٰلِدَىَّ وَأَنْ أَعْمَلَ صَٰلِحًا تَرْضَىٰهُ وَأَصْلِحْ لِى فِى
ذُرِّيَّتِىٓ ۖ إِنِّى تُبْتُ إِلَيْكَ وَإِنِّى مِنَ ٱلْمُسْلِمِينَ ﴿١٥﴾

"And We have enjoined upon man, to his parents, good treatment. His mother carried him with hardship and gave birth to him with hardship, and his gestation and weaning [period] is thirty months. [He grows] until, when he reaches maturity and reaches [the age of] forty years, he says, "My Lord, enable me to be grateful for Your favor which You have bestowed upon me and upon my parents and to work righteousness of which You will approve and make righteous for me my offspring. Indeed, I have repented to You, and indeed, I am of the Muslims."[155]

153. Al-Ankabut, Ayah 8
154. Luqman, Ayah 14
155. Al-Ahqaf, Ayah 15

The Quranic commandments further unfold through three additional verses, each commencing with the verb "وصى" (which can be translated as enjoin, command, or order). In its various forms and connotations, these verbs emphasize the vital significance of relaying the message of the Creator to humanity. Consequently, the information contained within these verses holds great value and should be implemented in our behavior and attitude toward our parents, with a particular emphasis on providing special care and consideration to mothers who often endure more hardships than fathers.

These verses illuminate mothers' profound and unconditional love for their children, their selfless and unrecompensed sacrifices, and the numerous trials and tribulations they endure. From the difficulties faced during pregnancy to the pains and illnesses experienced during childbirth, mothers bear the brunt of physical, psychological, and emotional challenges. These trials elevate their status to a level higher than that of fathers, as emphasized by the Prophet Muhammad ﷺ in an authentic narration recorded by Imam Muslim.

Abu Huraira reported that a person said:

« جاء رجل إلى رسول الله صلى الله عليه وسلم فقال: يا رسول الله من أحق الناس بحسن صحابتي؟

«قال: أمك، قال: ثم من؟ قال: ثم أمك، قال ثم من؟ قال: ثم أمك، قال: ثم من؟ قال: ثم أبوك» »

"Allah's Messenger, who amongst the people is most deserving of my good treatment? He said: Your mother, again your mother, again your mother, then your father, then your nearest relatives according to the order (of nearness)."[156]

Unsurprisingly, in the Books of Hadith, Abdullah Ibn Abbas has highlighted treating one's mother as the most virtuous deed in strengthening one's relationship with Allah. He profoundly expressed: He said:

« قال ابن عباس: لا أعلم عملاً أقرب إلى الله عز وجل من بر الوالدة »

"I know of no other deed that brings people closer to Allah than kind treatment and respect towards one's mother."[157]

The preceding evidence clearly demonstrates how Islam elevates the status of mothers to the highest level. The honor bestowed upon parents and, specifically, mothers in Islam surpasses that found in any other religion, ideology, or culture.

156. Muslim 2548.
157. Al-Adab al-Mufrad Bukhârî 1/45.

2.0 PARENTAL MORAL OBLIGATIONS TOWARD CHILDREN

2.1 Islamic perspective on parent-child relationships

A. Procreation as a Fulfillment of Shariah's Fundamental Objectives:

In Islam, one of Shariah's grand objectives is preserving life. This objective is actualized through the institution of marriage and the act of procreation, which serve as vital means for the continuation of human existence and survival. Recognizing children's lofty status in Islam, the religion encourages believers to embrace parenthood. The Messenger of Allah, ﷺ, urged men to seek out spouses who possess qualities of love and fertility, emphasizing the importance of having children as a means to fulfill this noble goal. On the authority of Anas Bin Malik, may Allah be pleased with him:

« جاء رجل إلى النبي صلى الله عليه وسلم, فقال: إني أصبت امرأة ذات حسب وجمال, وأنها لا تلد, أفأتزوجها قال: لا ثم أتاه الثانية فنهاه, ثم أتاه الثالثة , فقال: تزوجوا الولود الدود فإني مكاثر بكم الأمم »

A man came to the Prophet (صلى الله عليه وسلم) and said: I have found a woman of rank and beauty, but she does not give birth to children. Should I marry her? He said: No. He came again to him, but he prohibited him. He came to him the third time, and he (the Prophet) said: "Marry the one who is loving and fertile, for I shall outnumber the peoples by you."[158]

In contrast to the Western perception of children as burdensome, Islam holds a distinct perspective. Across Europe, modern birth control methods and population control measures have significantly declined fertility rates. According to the United Nations, the projected population of the EU block is expected to decrease from 446 million today to 365 million by 2100. While birth control has been practiced throughout history, some extreme measures, such as infanticide, have been employed as forms of population control. However, it is crucial to emphasize that Islam rejects such practices and upholds the value and protection of children. Poverty and the inability to provide for children should never be used as justifications for committing evil acts. [159]

B. Children are a blessing:

The Quranic teachings highlight the significance of acknowledging

158. Abu Daud 2050

159. Abdul Malik Sheikh explores the Islamic perspective on childhood and child protection in his work "Darul Iman Birmingham."Al-nasa'I 3227. Al-bani graded it as hasan saheeh.

and cherishing the gift of children to foster gratitude towards the Creator. Children are among the countless and immeasurable blessings bestowed upon humanity by Allah. As servants of Allah, it is our duty to express gratitude for these blessings, knowing that by doing so, we can experience their increase and continuity, as promised by Allah ﷻ in the Quran. Through our gratitude and responsible nurturing, we can ensure the perpetuation of this divine blessing in our lives and the lives of future generations.

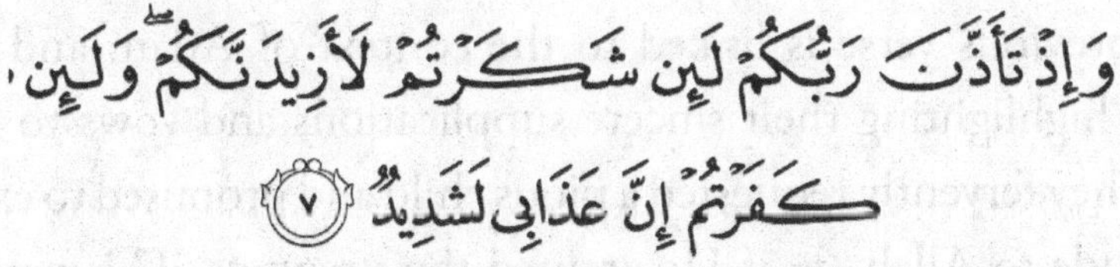

"And [remember] when your Lord proclaimed, 'If you are grateful, I will surely increase you [in favor]; but if you deny, indeed, My punishment is severe." [160]

In addition, it is mentioned in the Quran across various chapters that every blessing carries its own responsibility. The magnitude of a blessing directly correlates with the extent of responsibility placed upon us. We are held accountable by Allah ﷻ for each and every type of blessing bestowed upon us, irrespective of its scale or nature. Allah ﷻ states:

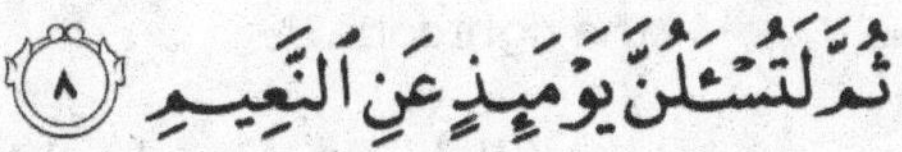

"Then you will surely be asked that Day about pleasure [161]

However, the Quran provides numerous instances where prophets

160. Ibrahim, 7
161. Al-Takathur, 8

and righteous individuals sought blessings from Allah ﷻ through their supplications and expressed profound gratitude upon receiving them. These verses exemplify different manifestations of seeking and appreciating blessings from Allah. Allah says:

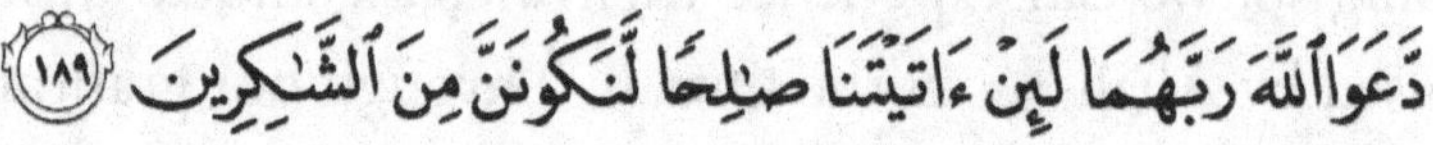

"they both invoke Allāh, their Lord, "If You should give us a good [] [child], we will surely be among the grateful" [162]

The previous verse is linked to the context of Adam and Eve's story, highlighting their sincere supplications and vows to Allah ﷻ. They fervently requested a pious child and promised to express gratitude to Allah ﷻ if He granted their request. This narrative emphasizes that children are indeed a blessing that warrants deep appreciation and thankfulness towards Allah ﷻ.

It also reads in Quran:

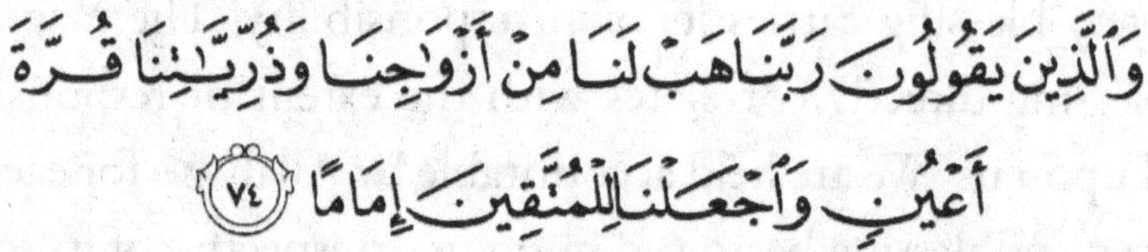

"And those who say, "Our Lord, grant us from among our wives and offspring comfort to our eyes and make us an example for the righteous." [163]

Prophet Abraham praising Allah ﷻ for the blessing, Quranic states:

162. Al-Araf 432
163. Al-Furqan, Ayah 74

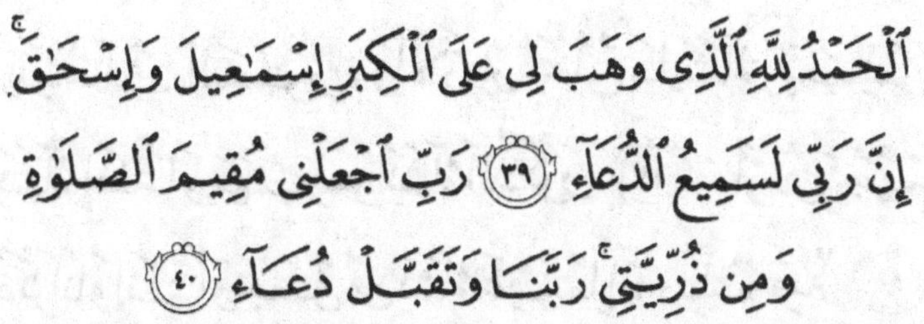

«Praise to Allah, who has granted to me in old age Ishmael and Isaac. Indeed, my Lord is the Hearer of supplication.
My Lord, make me an establisher of prayer, and [many] from my descendants. Our Lord, and accept my supplication" [164]

Upon close examination of the verses above, the Quran portrays children as a source of comfort to the eyes and a gift that Allah ﷻ can only bestow in response to sincere supplication offered by His servants. This is exemplified in verse 74 of Al-Furqan, where the pious servants of Allah ﷻ express their desire to be granted righteous offspring as solace in their eyes. Additionally, we see the case of Prophet Abraham, who fervently prayed to Allah ﷻ despite his old age and expressed gratitude when he was blessed with his beloved sons, Ishmael and Isaac.

Furthermore, the Quran provides clarification regarding the gender of a child. It affirms that while Allah ﷻ holds the authority to determine and select the gender, His servants are granted the freedom to express their desires through supplication. However, it is essential to recognize that the ultimate decision rests with Allah ﷻ alone.

The Quran states:

164. Ibrahim, Ayah 39 – 40

لِّلَّهِ مُلْكُ ٱلسَّمَٰوَٰتِ وَٱلْأَرْضِ ۚ يَخْلُقُ مَا يَشَآءُ ۚ يَهَبُ لِمَن يَشَآءُ إِنَٰثًا وَيَهَبُ لِمَن يَشَآءُ ٱلذُّكُورَ ﴿٤٩﴾ أَوْ يُزَوِّجُهُمْ ذُكْرَانًا وَإِنَٰثًا ۖ وَيَجْعَلُ مَن يَشَآءُ عَقِيمًا ۚ إِنَّهُۥ عَلِيمٌ قَدِيرٌ ﴿٥٠﴾

"To Allāh belongs the dominion of the heavens and the earth; He creates what He wills. He gives to whom He wills female [children], and He gives to whom He wills males" "Or He makes them [both] males and females, and He renders whom He wills barren. Indeed, He is Knowing and Competent". [165]

The verse above highlights that the selection of a child's gender is solely in the hands of Allah ﷻ. It is He who determines whether the child will be male or female, and He alone has the power to bestow fertility or infertility upon individuals.

As believers, we should joyfully embrace the gift bestowed by Allah ﷻ, irrespective of the child's gender, recognizing that the ultimate decision rests with Allah's wisdom and choice. However, the act of despising daughters and engaging in discriminatory behavior towards them is a repugnant practice rooted in the Days of Ignorance. It reflects a lack of understanding of religious teachings and indicates a weakness in one's faith.

The Quran draws attention to this regressive custom in two verses from separate chapters, highlighting the disturbing practice of devaluing and even burying newborn daughters alive during the era of ignorance.

The first verse in surat Al-Nahl:

165. Al-Shura 49-50

وَإِذَا بُشِّرَ أَحَدُهُم بِٱلۡأُنثَىٰ ظَلَّ وَجۡهُهُۥ مُسۡوَدّٗا وَهُوَ كَظِيمٞ ﴿٥٨﴾
يَتَوَٰرَىٰ مِنَ ٱلۡقَوۡمِ مِن سُوٓءِ مَا بُشِّرَ بِهِۦٓۚ أَيُمۡسِكُهُۥ عَلَىٰ هُونٍ أَمۡ يَدُ
سُّهُۥ فِي ٱلتُّرَابِۗ أَلَا سَآءَ مَا يَحۡكُمُونَ ﴿٥٩﴾

"..And when one of them is informed of [the birth of] a female, his face becomes dark, and he suppresses grief.

He hides himself from the people because of the ill of which he has been informed. Should he keep it in humiliation or bury it in the ground? Unquestionably, evil is what they decide". 166

And again, in surat Al-Zukhruh:

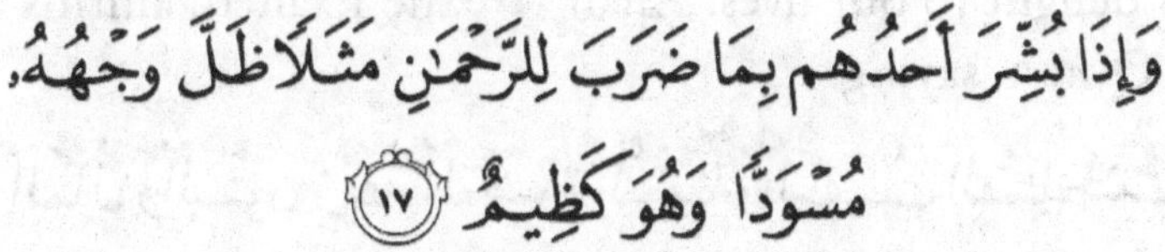

"..And when one of them is given good tidings of that which he attributes to the Most Merciful in comparison, his face becomes dark, and he suppresses grief". 167

In order to reject the habit that Islam strongly condemns, it is imperative that we practice fairness and equality in our treatment of both sons and daughters. Taking care of our daughters and giving them proper attention fulfills our duties and holds a special reward, as promised by the Prophet Muhammad ﷺ. He assured us that those who raise their daughters with love and compassion will be granted the companionship of the Prophet in Paradise in the hereafter. This serves as a profound encouragement to value

166. An-Nahl, Ayah 58 -59
167. Az-Zukhruf, Ayah 17

and nurture our daughters with utmost care. Anas رضي الله عنه reported: The Prophet ﷺ said:

« من أعال جاريتين »بنتين« حتى تبلغا جاء يوم القيامة أنا وهو وضم أصابعه »

"Whoever supports two girls till they attain maturity, he and I will come on the Day of Resurrection (close to each other) like this –The Messenger of Allah joined his fingers to illustrate closeness."[168]

C. Children are adornment. Children are indeed a source of beauty and happiness in this world. They bring immense joy and delight to our lives. Allah ﷻ, the Exalted, affirms this in the Quran, saying:

ٱلْمَالُ وَٱلْبَنُونَ زِينَةُ ٱلْحَيَوٰةِ ٱلدُّنْيَا ۖ وَٱلْبَٰقِيَٰتُ ٱلصَّٰلِحَٰتُ خَيْرٌ عِندَ رَبِّكَ ثَوَابًا وَخَيْرٌ أَمَلًا ﴿٤٦﴾

"Wealth and children are [but] adornment of the worldly life" [169]

زُيِّنَ لِلنَّاسِ حُبُّ ٱلشَّهَوَٰتِ مِنَ ٱلنِّسَآءِ وَٱلْبَنِينَ وَٱلْقَنَٰطِيرِ ٱلْمُقَنطَرَةِ مِنَ ٱلذَّهَبِ وَٱلْفِضَّةِ وَٱلْخَيْلِ ٱلْمُسَوَّمَةِ وَٱلْأَنْعَٰمِ وَٱلْحَرْثِ ۗ ذَٰلِكَ مَتَٰعُ ٱلْحَيَوٰةِ ٱلدُّنْيَا ۖ وَٱللَّهُ عِندَهُۥ حُسْنُ ٱلْمَـَٔابِ ﴿١٤﴾

«Beautified for people is the love of that which they desire - of women and sons, heaped-up sums of gold and silver, fine

168. Muslim 2631
169. Al-kahf, 46

branded horses, and cattle and tilled land. That is the enjoyment of worldly life, but Allah has with Him the best return".[170]

The love for offspring is undeniably one of the most cherished pleasures of this worldly life. It is intertwined with other enjoyable aspects such as wealth, luxurious possessions like horses, fertile lands, and livestock, collectively encompassing the sum of worldly delights. Nevertheless, parents' love for children is an innate and natural inclination to care for them, show kindness, and display compassion. It is a beautiful adornment of the world. Without this inherent love and motivation, humanity could have faced extinction.

Essentially, these verses offer advice to prioritize the rewards and blessings of the Hereafter over those of the worldly life. Furthermore, these verses compare the temporary pleasures of this world that entice people and the everlasting pleasure of the Hereafter. They caution believers against becoming captivated by worldly comforts and desires.

"All these desires and similar ones are the fleeting comforts of this life. It is worth noting that the term 'this life' or 'dunyā' in the Arabic text signifies 'the lower life.' Therefore, these comforts do not pertain to the sublime and higher realm. They are merely the easy delights of the worldly life. What surpasses all these pleasures, both in nobility and in safeguarding the human soul from being consumed by worldly desires, is that which is eternal and remains with God."[171]

170. Al-E-Imran, Ayah 14
171. Zilal Al-Quran, Surat Al-Imran, Verse 14

D. Children are فتنة trail:

Besides being an adornment and a blessing, children can also be a test or trial, as mentioned in the Quran. Allah addresses this aspect, saying:

وَٱعۡلَمُوٓاْ أَنَّمَآ أَمۡوَٰلُكُمۡ وَأَوۡلَٰدُكُمۡ فِتۡنَةٞ وَأَنَّ ٱللَّهَ عِندَهُۥٓ أَجۡرٌ عَظِيمٞ ٢٨

"And know that your properties and your children are but a trial and that Allāh has with Him a great reward." [172]

The mentioned verse emphasizes that when Allah ﷻ blesses us with children, it serves as a test to assess how parents will fulfill their responsibilities in raising them. It examines the sincerity with which parents adhere to Islamic principles of nurturing (Tarbiyah), such as displaying kindness, love, and respect towards their children. It also evaluates parents' readiness to establish a faith-centered and morally grounded environment that connects their children to their Creator, thereby equipping them for the challenges of the Hereafter and ensuring their preparedness for Paradise.

E. Children are a trust

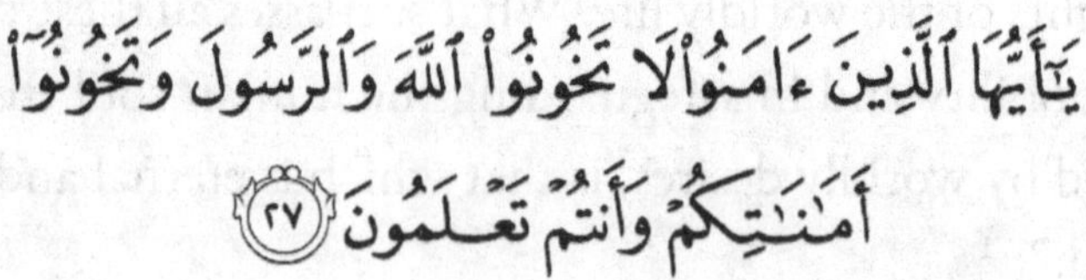

172. Al-Anfal, 28

O you who have believed, do not betray Allah and the Messenger or betray your trusts while you know [the consequence]. [173]

Allah ﷻ, in His honor, has blessed us with sons and daughters as a means of testing and trial. This trial examines whether we will fulfill our responsibilities towards them, which include caring for them, providing guidance, imparting knowledge, and nurturing their character. It measures whether we will diligently fulfill this trust or neglect it, wasting the opportunity and obligation given to us.

The Quran extensively praises the qualities of the believers whose faith and salvation are affirmed by fulfilling this sacred trust. These believers are recognized for their commitment to upholding the Amanah (the trust) bestowed upon them. This is evident at the beginning of Surah al-Mu'minun, where Allah highlights the attributes of those whose faith is genuine and steadfast. Allah said:

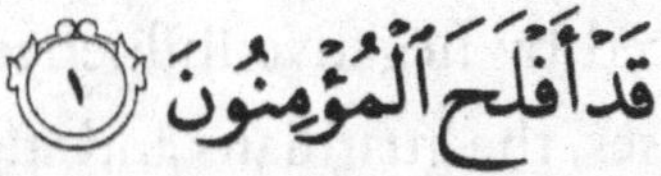

«Certainly, will the believers have succeeded" [174]

Furthermore, in subsequent verses, those who attained success are described as individuals who possess the quality of trustworthiness:

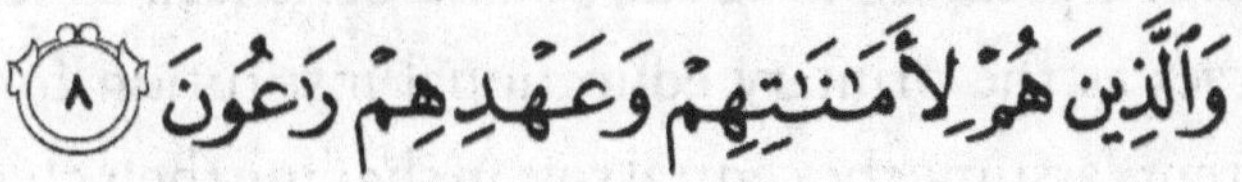

"And they who are to their trusts and their promises attentive." [175]

173. Al-Anfal, Ayah 27
174. Al- Mu'minun 1
175. Al-Mu'minun, Ayah 8

According to Al-Imam Ghazali, the child is regarded as a trust from Allah ﷻ bestowed upon parents. He beautifully describes the purity and malleability of a child's heart, comparing it to an uncut jewel that can be shaped and influenced in various ways. The child's heart is likened to a simple mirror that can absorb and reflect the impressions and influences it receives.

Al-Ghazali further emphasizes the crucial role of parents and caregivers in guiding and instructing the child. They are responsible for nurturing the child towards true success in both this world and the hereafter. The upbringing and instruction provided by parents greatly influence the child's future actions and choices. Whether the child ultimately succeeds or fails, the parents and all those who contribute to the child's guidance and education will share in the outcome.

Conversely, neglecting their moral development and allowing them to be influenced by negative influences can lead to misery and ruin. In such cases, the guardians and supervisors of the child bear the responsibility for the negative outcome.[176]

F. Children are a responsibility:

Islam places significant emphasis on nurturing children in a manner that is pleasing to Allah ﷻ and beneficial to society. The home serves as the primary educational institution for children, where parents assume the central role in shaping their character and establishing the initial foundation of their personalities. Parents are responsible for instilling moral values and teaching etiquettes that enable children to discern between right and wrong, good and

176. Al-Ghazali, Ihya Ulumudeen vol:2 page: 70

evil, and what is lawful (Halal) and unlawful (Haram).

Due to their vital role in children's upbringing, parents are held accountable for their crucial duty of tarbiyah (nurturing and upbringing). Allah addresses this responsibility in the Quran, emphasizing the significance of the parent's role.

يَٰٓأَيُّهَا ٱلَّذِينَ ءَامَنُوا۟ قُوٓا۟ أَنفُسَكُمْ وَأَهْلِيكُمْ نَارًا وَقُودُهَا ٱلنَّاسُ
وَٱلْحِجَارَةُ عَلَيْهَا مَلَٰٓئِكَةٌ غِلَاظٌ شِدَادٌ لَّا يَعْصُونَ ٱللَّهَ مَآ
أَمَرَهُمْ وَيَفْعَلُونَ مَا يُؤْمَرُونَ ٦

"O you who have believed, protect yourselves and your families from a Fire whose fuel is people and stones, over which are [appointed] angels, harsh and severe; they do not disobey Allah in what He commands them but do what they are commanded."[177]

وَأْمُرْ أَهْلَكَ بِٱلصَّلَوٰةِ وَٱصْطَبِرْ عَلَيْهَا ۖ لَا نَسْـَٔلُكَ رِزْقًا ۖ نَّحْنُ
نَرْزُقُكَ ۗ وَٱلْعَٰقِبَةُ لِلتَّقْوَىٰ ١٣٢

"And enjoin prayer upon your family [and people] and be steadfast therein. We ask you not for provision; We provide for you, and the [best] outcome is for [those of] righteousness".[178]

وَكَانَ يَأْمُرُ أَهْلَهُۥ بِٱلصَّلَوٰةِ وَٱلزَّكَوٰةِ وَكَانَ عِندَ رَبِّهِۦ مَرْضِيًّا ٥٥

"And he used to enjoin on his people prayer and zakah and was to his Lord pleasing."[179]

177. At-Tahrim, Ayah 6
178. Ta-Ha, Ayah 132
179. Maryam, Ayah 55

The aforementioned Quranic verses highlight that a crucial aspect of raising children, which is a profound responsibility and noble task for parents, is establishing a strong connection between the children and their Creator, Allah ﷻ.

A comprehensive approach must be adopted to nurture children in the spirit of religion, particularly focusing on their Aqeedah (belief system), as beliefs guide actions. It involves fostering Imaan (faith) and Taqwa (God-consciousness) within their hearts. Only when children are taught to wholeheartedly submit to Allah ﷻ in their thoughts, words, and actions can they be expected to exert their utmost efforts to please Him.

It is essential for children to develop a love for Allah ﷻ that surpasses their love for any other person or worldly possession. By nurturing children with good morals, parents lay the foundation for their spiritual and ethical growth.

Authentic narrations Throughout Islamic teachings emphasize the significance of cultivating children with virtuous morals. Some of these narrations serve as guidance in this noble endeavor.

a- On the authority of Amr Bin Al-As, in which the prophet ﷺ said:

« ما نَحل والدٌ ولدَه من نحْل أفضل من أدب حسَن »

"No father can give his child anything better than good manners."[180]

b- In a narration Ibnu Umar, prophet ﷺ said:

180. Tirmidi 1952 and Ahmed 4/77-78

« كلكم راع وكلكم مسؤول عن رعيته: الإمام راع ومسئول عن رعيته، والرجل راع في أهله ومسئول عن رعيته، والمرأة راعية في بيت زوجها ومسئولة عن»رعيتها» وقال - صلى الله عليه وسلم -: »إن الله سائل كل راع عما استرعاه أحفظ، أم ضيع؟ حتى يسأل الرجل عن أهل بيته» »

"All of you are shepherds, and each is responsible for his flock; The man is the guardian of the family of his household and is responsible for his subjects, and the woman is the guardian of her husband's home and his children and is responsible for them."[181] In another version by the same companion, may Allah be pleased with him, the prophet said: "Allah will ask everyone about what he had entrusted with so much so that the man will be asked about his household."[182]

As stated earlier, the narrations underscore the critical and paramount responsibility of parenting. It highlights that parents should prioritize not only the immediate nurturing and protection of their children in this worldly life but also focus on preparing them for the future. This broader perspective encourages parents to consider their children's long-term development and growth beyond the present moment.

c- Ibnu Umar also said:

« أدب ابنك فإنك مسئول عنه ، ماذا أدبته وماذا علمته ؟ وهو مسئول عن برك وطواعيته لك»

"Discipline your child, for verily; you are responsible for him on

181. Sahih al-Bukhari 5188

182. Al-Nasa'I 292 and Al-tirmidi 4/180, and Sh Al-Bani approved its conformity to the saheeh standards

the Day of Judgement: with what did you discipline him and what did you teach him?"[183]

Abdullah Ibn 'Umar, the narrator of the hadiths mentioned above, further expounded on the significance of the meaning he conveyed and how the responsibility of nurturing children should be fulfilled. He emphasized that on the Day of Judgment, we will be held accountable before Allah ﷻ for how we have discharged this responsibility, including whether we have disciplined and guided our children appropriately.

Indeed, parenting holds immense importance in Islam, to the extent that on the Day of Judgment, Allah ﷻ will first inquire from the child about the effectiveness of the parent before questioning the parent regarding the child's obedience. This highlights the weightiness and magnitude of the parental role in shaping the lives and character of their children.

G. Children are innately born with fitrah (natural inclination towards righteousness):

On the authority of Abu Huraira, the prophet ﷺ, said:

«مَا مِنْ مَوْلُودٍ إِلاَّ يُولَدُ عَلَى الْفِطْرَةِ فَأَبَوَاهُ يُهَوِّدَانِهِ وَيُنَصِّرَانِهِ وَيُمَجِّسَانِهِ كَمَا تُنْتَجُ الْبَهِيمَةُ بَهِيمَةً جَمْعَاءَ هَلْ تُحِسُّونَ فِيهَا مِنْ جَدْعَاءَ» ثُمَّ يَقُولُ أَبُو هُرَيْرَةَ : وَاقْرَءُوا إِنْ شِئْتُمْ فطرة الله التي فطر الناس عليها لا تبديل لخلق الله »

«There is none born but is created to his true nature (Islam). It is his parents who make him a Jew or a Christian or a Magian quite as beasts produce their young with their limbs perfect.

183. Al-Sunan Al-Kubra of Al-Bayhaqi 1035

> Do you see anything deficient in them? Then he quoted the Qur›an., The nature made by Allah in which He has created men, there is no altering of Allah›s creation; that is the right religion.»[184]

Al-Imam Al-Nawawi elaborating on the breadth and depth of the meaning of this narration, said: The majority of Muslim scholars have reached a consensus that when children from the Muslims pass away, they are considered among the inhabitants of Jannah (Paradise) as they are not held accountable due to their young age and lack of legal responsibility.

Some who did not hold this position refrained from taking such a definitive stance due to the hadith of Aaishah, to which the scholars respond that perhaps he ﷺ wanted to prevent her from rushing to a definitive conclusion without having had definitive evidence to support it, just as he corrected Sa'd ibn Abi Waqqaas when he said, "Verily I see him be a mu'min," so he ﷺ said, "or a Muslim." And perhaps he ﷺ said this before he knew that the children of Muslims are in Jannah, for it is known that he ﷺ said, "Any Muslim who loses three children before they reach the age of maturity will be granted Jannah by Allah ﷻ, the Exalted, out of His Mercy for them" and elsewhere in other hadith narrations. And Allah ﷻ knows best".[185]

In this narration, the Prophet ﷺ affirms that children are born with an innate belief in Allah ﷻ, the Almighty, and an inclination towards the pure monotheistic Aqeedah (belief system). What

184. Ar-Rum:30, Muslim 2658

185. Al-Nawawi, Sharh Saheeh Muslim vol:16 page 261. The translated by Tulayha word press 8/9/2013

a child absorbs, whether good or evil, plays a significant role in shaping their character as they grow older. It is their surroundings and environmental factors that can potentially influence them negatively. Hence, the role of guardians, especially parents, becomes vital in raising children free from moral corruption and deviation from the path of the Deen (religion).

Parents are profoundly responsible for safeguarding and nurturing their children's Fitrah (natural disposition) and preventing its decline and degradation. They are also tasked with being exemplary role models, as failing to do so can have a detrimental impact on their children's morality.

Regrettably, what Ibn al-Qayim highlighted is observable in our world today, as too many parents fail this test. Muslim parents, in particular, are missing out on the exceptional opportunity for eternal and spiritual rewards by neglecting their children and falling short in this duty.

Ibnul Qayim stressing the significance of the stage of upbringing, said: "How many people had caused misery to their own children, the apple of their eyes, in this world-life and the Afterlife, by neglecting them, not disciplining them, encouraging them to follow their whims and desires, thinking that they were honoring them when they were humiliating them, that they were being merciful to them when in fact they were wronging them They have not benefited from having a child, and they have made the child lose his share in this worldly life and the Afterlife. If you think about children's corruption, you will see that in most cases, it is because of the parents."[186]

It is disheartening to observe that Ibn al-Qayim's observation holds true in our present world, as many parents fail in their responsibility. This failure is particularly significant among Muslim parents who miss out on the excellent opportunity for eternal and spiritual rewards by neglecting their children and falling short in this test.

The prophet Muhammad ﷺ clearly demonstrated the critical role of parents in shaping their offspring's moral character and overall personality and emphasized it by Himself. An authentic hadith highlights the profound significance of parental care and attitudes in transforming a child, regardless of their innate nature, attributes, and disposition at birth. No child is born as an armed robber, a drug addict, or a prostitute, just as no one is born trustworthy, law-abiding, or a peacemaker. These traits develop and evolve throughout life, greatly influenced by the environment in which one grows up. It is through the permission and guidance of the Almighty that the environment molds and shapes us into whom we become[187]

H. Children are a source of reward for parents:

Believers have a profound obligation to strive for good deeds in order to attain Allah's pleasure. However, considering the brevity of life, it becomes challenging to achieve a significant amount of good in the limited time allotted to individuals. In His wisdom, Allah has provided believers with alternative opportunities

186. Al-Imam ibn al-Qayyim Tuhfat al-Mawdūd bi-Ahkām il-Mawlūd, Page 146
187. (Dr. Abdul-Razzaq Abdul-Majeed Alaro, "Children Moral Upbringing: The Shariah Recipe," Allawh Journal of Arabic and Islamic Studies, University of Maiduguri, Maiduguri, Nigeria, 1st June 2017).

through their offspring, enabling the continuation of rewards both during the parents' lifetime and after their departure from this world. This is especially significant as parents considerably require these rewards for salvation from hellfire and elevation to higher ranks in heaven.

The Prophet Muhammad ﷺ has conveyed three beautiful narrations that affirm the reality mentioned above, and these narrations hold true according to the standards of authenticity set by the scholars of Hadith. These narrations bring great glad tidings to the believers, serving as a source of encouragement and motivation in their journey towards righteousness and the pursuit of eternal rewards.

He said :

- Abu Hurairah reported that the Messenger of Allah ﷺ said:

« إذا مات ابن آدم انقطع عمله إلا من ثلاث صدقة جارية أو علم ينتفع به أو ولد صالح يدعو له »

"When a man dies, his deeds come to an end, except for three: A continuous charity, knowledge by which people derive benefit, a pious son who prays for him." 188

- Allah's Messenger said, as reported by Abu Huraira:

«الْقِنْطَارُ اثْنَا عَشَرَ أَلْفَ أُوقِيَّةٍ كُلُّ أُوقِيَّةٍ خَيْرٌ مِمَّا بَيْنَ السَّمَاءِ وَالأَرْضِ». وَقَالَ رَسُولُ اللَّهِ ـ صلى الله عليه وسلم ـ «إِنَّ الرَّجُلَ لَتُرْفَعُ دَرَجَتُهُ فِي الْجَنَّةِ فَيَقُولُ أَنَّى هَذَا فَيُقَالُ

188. Muslim Book 7, Hadith 94

بِاسْتِغْفَارِ وَلَدِكَ لَكَ» »

"Qintar is twelve thousand 'Uqiyah, each 'Uqiyah of which is better than what is between heaven and earth." And the Messenger of Allah ﷺ said: "A man will be raised in status in Paradise and will say: 'Where did this come from?' And it will be said:'From your son's praying for forgiveness for you."[189]

Both narrations highlight the profound significance of obedient children in providing lasting good deeds for their parents through supplication.

– On the authority of Abu Musa Al-Asha'ri, the Messenger of Allah ﷺ said:

« «إذا مات ولد العبد قال الله تعالى لملائكته: قبضتم ولد عبدي؟ فيقولون : نَعَمْ ، فيقول : قَبَضْتُمْ ثَمَرَةَ فُؤادِهِ ؟ فيقولون : نَعَمْ ، فيقول : فماذا قال عبدي؟ فيقولون: حمدك واسترجع، فيقول الله تعالى: ابنوا لعبدي بيتًا في الجنة، وسموه بيت الحمد». رواه الترمذي وقال حديث حسن. »

"When a slave's child dies, Allah, the Most High, asks His angels, 'Have you taken out the life of the child of My slave?" They reply in the affirmative. He then asks, 'Have you taken the fruit of his heart?' They reply in the affirmative. Thereupon he asks, 'What has My slave said?' They say: 'He has praised You and said: Inna lillahi wa inna ilaihi raji'un (We belong to Allah and to Him we shall be returned). Allah says: 'Build a house for My slave in Jannah and name it as Bait-ul-Hamd' (the House of Praise)[190]

The previous narrations provide us with valuable insights, from

189. Ibnu Majah 3660, Book 33 Hadith 4
190. Al-bani, Silsialtu Al-Ahadeeth Al-Saheehah vol 3 page: 482

which we can infer the following points:

- Serve as a reminder that obedient and righteous children can contribute to their parents' record of good deeds. Through their sincere supplications and prayers, children can continue to benefit their parents even after passing. This is a source of immense comfort and hope for parents as their children become a means of endless blessings and rewards in this world and the Hereafter.

- Emphasize the importance of nurturing and raising children in a way that instills obedience to Allah and righteousness. By doing so, parents fulfill their responsibility towards their children's upbringing and create a lasting legacy of good deeds that can benefit them in the realm of the unseen.

- The narrations are also a powerful reminder of the potential impact of a child's piety and prayers on their parents' spiritual journey, encouraging believers to strive for the upbringing and guidance of their children in the best possible manner.

Moreover, The third Hadith narrated by Abu Musa illustrates that if a child passes away during the lifetime of their parents, the child will intercede for their parents, granting them entry into Paradise. Similarly, the Hadith is uniquely a profound reminder of the mercy and intercession that can come from the loss of a child. It highlights the special status and intercessory role a departed child can have on behalf of their parents. The child's innocence, purity, and righteous state serve as a means of attaining Paradise for the grieving parents. On the other hand, it offers solace to parents who have experienced the loss of a child, assuring them that their departed child holds a unique position in the sight of Allah ﷻ. It serves as a source of hope and comfort, reassuring that their beloved child will advocate on their behalf on the Day of Judgment.

Understanding these narrations encourages parents to cherish their children and nurture them in accordance with Islamic teachings. It emphasizes the importance of fostering a loving and righteous environment that promotes their spiritual growth and well-being.

3.0 MORAL PARENTING COMPASS IN THE QURAN (MORAL CODES)

3.1 The role of parents in child moral upbringing in islam

A. The Story of Luqman and His Son

The Moral Upbringing Code in Verses 13-19 of Surah Luqman

Regarding the well-known story of Luqman and his guidance on child-raising in the Quran, Allah states:

وَإِذْ قَالَ لُقْمَٰنُ لِٱبْنِهِۦ وَهُوَ يَعِظُهُۥ يَٰبُنَيَّ لَا تُشْرِكْ بِٱللَّهِ إِنَّ
ٱلشِّرْكَ لَظُلْمٌ عَظِيمٌ ﴿١٣﴾ وَوَصَّيْنَا ٱلْإِنسَٰنَ بِوَٰلِدَيْهِ
حَمَلَتْهُ أُمُّهُۥ وَهْنًا عَلَىٰ وَهْنٍ وَفِصَٰلُهُۥ فِى عَامَيْنِ أَنِ ٱشْكُرْ

لِي وَلِوَٰلِدَيۡكَ إِلَيَّ ٱلۡمَصِيرُ ١٤ وَإِن جَٰهَدَاكَ عَلَىٰٓ أَن تُشۡرِكَ
بِي مَا لَيۡسَ لَكَ بِهِۦ عِلۡمٞ فَلَا تُطِعۡهُمَاۖ وَصَاحِبۡهُمَا فِي ٱلدُّ
نۡيَا مَعۡرُوفٗاۖ وَٱتَّبِعۡ سَبِيلَ مَنۡ أَنَابَ إِلَيَّۚ ثُمَّ إِلَيَّ مَرۡجِعُكُمۡ
فَأُنَبِّئُكُم بِمَا كُنتُمۡ تَعۡمَلُونَ ١٥

يَٰبُنَيَّ إِنَّهَآ إِن تَكُ مِثۡقَالَ حَبَّةٖ مِّنۡ خَرۡدَلٖ فَتَكُن فِي صَخۡرَةٍ
أَوۡ فِي ٱلسَّمَٰوَٰتِ أَوۡ فِي ٱلۡأَرۡضِ يَأۡتِ بِهَا ٱللَّهُۚ إِنَّ ٱللَّهَ لَطِيفٌ
خَبِيرٞ ١٦ يَٰبُنَيَّ أَقِمِ ٱلصَّلَوٰةَ وَأۡمُرۡ بِٱلۡمَعۡرُوفِ وَٱنۡهَ عَنِ
ٱلۡمُنكَرِ وَٱصۡبِرۡ عَلَىٰ مَآ أَصَابَكَۖ إِنَّ ذَٰلِكَ مِنۡ عَزۡمِ ٱلۡأُمُورِ ١٧
وَلَا تُصَعِّرۡ خَدَّكَ لِلنَّاسِ وَلَا تَمۡشِ فِي ٱلۡأَرۡضِ مَرَحًاۖ إِنَّ ٱللَّهَ لَا يُحِبُّ كُلَّ
مُخۡتَالٖ فَخُورٖ ١٨ وَٱقۡصِدۡ فِي مَشۡيِكَ وَٱغۡضُضۡ مِن صَوۡتِكَۚ
إِنَّ أَنكَرَ ٱلۡأَصۡوَٰتِ لَصَوۡتُ ٱلۡحَمِيرِ ١٩

«And [mention, O Muhammad], when Luqman said to his son while he was instructing him, «O my son, do not associate [anything] with Allah. Indeed, association [with Him] is great injustice. And We have enjoined upon man [care] for his parents. His mother carried him, [increasing her] in weakness upon weakness, and his weaning is in two years. Be grateful to Me and to your parents; to Me is the [final] destination. But if they endeavor to make you associate with Me that of which you have no knowledge, do not obey them but accompany them in [this] world with appropriate kindness and follow the way of those who turn back to Me [in repentance]. Then to Me will be your return, and I will inform you about what you

> used to do. [And Luqman said], «O my son, indeed if wrong should be the weight of a mustard seed and should be within a rock or [anywhere] in the heavens or in the earth, Allah will bring it forth. Indeed, Allah is Subtle and Acquainted. "O my son, establish prayer, enjoin what is right, forbid what is wrong, and be patient over what befalls you. Indeed, [all] that is of the matters [requiring] determination. And do not turn your cheek [in contempt] toward people and do not walk through the earth exultantly. Indeed, Allah does not like everyone self-deluded and boastful. And be moderate in your pace and lower your voice; indeed, the most disagreeable of sounds is the voice of donkeys." [191]

By contemplating this long Quranic passage that contains the fundamental principles of the Islamic method of upbringing children, we learn that Luqman, in his preaching and speech with his son, left no vital tarbiyyah item unexplained. His wise and beautiful words, which to this day echo in the ears of millions of people, covered all the significant foundations of Tarbiyah, ranging from monotheism down to a detailed and practical-individual and social-based-moral code of Islamic Tarbiyah.

Accordingly, his walk-talk speech can be summarized in seven main categories, which are as follows:

- **(Verse 13) The prohibition of Shirk as a "great injustice**."

Tawheed is the basis of all that is in Islam. It should be introduced to children at an early age. Neglecting this essential principle of Islam can cause children to have doubts and unanswered questions that preoccupy their minds. Teaching them tawheed means maintaining the fitrah with which the children were born.

191. Luqman, Ayah 13 -19

In his advice to his son, Luqman warned him against shirk, the worst and the greatest sin ever committed by human beings on earth. Every prophet or messenger warned his nation against shirk or associating with Allah others, which is injustice concerning the rights of Allah ﷻ upon His servants.

If parents skip this critical part of the deen, Tawheed, and concentrate on the other practical aspects of Islam, the fruits we reap from our long struggle with upbringing them Islamicly will end up in vain.

- **(Verse 14) Good treatment towards parents;** the weaknesses a mother bears when she carries her child and breastfeeding him for two years; being grateful to Allah and parents.

Luqman alerted his son on obedience to the parents with a particular focus on the mother since she has more rights than the father, as discussed earlier in this book in the chapter on moralities with the parents.

- **(Verse 15) Not to follow one's parents if they call towards shirk;** to do well with them well in this world; and to follow the path of the one who turns towards Allah (whomever it might be), because the final return is to Allah, Who will then inform us of all that we did.

Parents deserve to be respected and must always be obeyed at all times except when their obedience leads to the disobedience of Allah and His prophet, ﷺ; when they call to shirk or associate with Allah others, then they are not to be obeyed in the such matter though the good treatment remains as it is.

- **(Verse 16) Allah ﷻ knows every little thing,** where ever it might be in the Heavens and the earth, and He will bring it forth. Luqman tries to inculcate in the heart of his son the surveillance of Allah, The Almighty, and his watchfulness over His creatures where Allah observers the inns and the outs of every creature in every space and time, a potential and a meaningful item of Tarbiyah that teaches the child the integrity and being God-conscious in all his actions and sayings, and intentions and thinking.
- **(Verse 17) Among the pieces of Luqman's wisdom to his son was the Establishment of prayer**, commanding what is good, prohibiting what is evil, and remaining patient in facing what happens while doing these three things, which requires determination. This part of Luqman's golden advice is more practical than the pieces of wisdom mentioned earlier as it touches on the most important pillar of Islam after Tawheed, prayer. Similarly, it lays down another essential principle of guidance for the Muslims to invite others to keep to the true faith and good deeds as necessary as their submission to the Holy Qur'an and Sunnah. Without sincere efforts, to the best of one's ability, to invite others to the right path, one's good deeds are not enough for one's salvation. Especially if a person does not take care of the spiritual and moral welfare of his wife, children, and family and turns a blind eye to their unrighteous deeds, he is blocking his way to salvation - no matter how pious he might be. Therefore, the Qur'an and the Sunnah make it obligatory for every Muslim to do his best to invite others to the good deeds and warn them against evil acts.

Furthermore, being patient in the cause of implementing the principles of da'wa is a primary requirement while serving Islam. See Ma'rif-ul-Quran, Surat Al-Asr.

- **(Verses 18) Not turning one's cheek towards people (in contempt),** not strutting about on earth (arrogantly) because Allah ﷻ does not love the vainglorious boaster. "In verse 18, it was said: وَلَا تُصَعِّرْ خَدَّكَ لِلنَّاسِ (And do not turn your cheek away from people). The expression: لَا تُصَعِّرْ (la tusa"ir) is a derivation from صَعَرَ (sa' ara), which is a disease among camels that causes a tilt in the neck similar to the stroke among human beings that makes a face crooked. It carries the sense of turning one's face away (in disdain). Thus, the verse means: 'Do not turn your face away from people when you meet them and talk to them for it is a sign of avoidance and arrogance and very much against the norms of gentle manners".[192]

  In addition, he warned his son against being arrogant while walking, a bad habit that Allah hates.

- **(Verse 19)Being moderate in one's gait and keeping one's voice low**, as the most disliked of all voices, is the braying of the ass. In lowering one's voice, one shows good manners with people and Allah. "Had there been any merit in the loud, harsh, shrill voice, the donkey would not be singled out with such a voice; the donkey's baseness and stupidity are well-known. Furthermore, it is disrespectful to others when they are spoken in that manner of harshness."[193]

192. Ibid
193. Fuad Ibn Abdul- Azeez Asha-Shaulboob, the book of Manners, page:180,

B. Nuh and his son:

The Moral Upbringing Code in Verses 41-47 of surat hud. (nuh and his son)

Allah ﷻ narrates the story of Nuh (Noah) and his son in Surah Hud, the only chapter in the Quran explicitly mentioning this particular historical incident not found in any other part of the Quran.

- Verses 41-44

Allah ﷻ says:

۞ وَقَالَ ٱرۡكَبُواْ فِيهَا بِسۡمِ ٱللَّهِ مَجۡرٜىٰهَا وَمُرۡسَىٰهَآۚ إِنَّ رَبِّي
لَغَفُورٞ رَّحِيمٞ ﴿٤١﴾ وَهِيَ تَجۡرِي بِهِمۡ فِي مَوۡجٖ كَٱلۡجِبَالِ وَنَادَىٰ
نُوحٌ ٱبۡنَهُۥ وَكَانَ فِي مَعۡزِلٖ يَٰبُنَيَّ ٱرۡكَب مَّعَنَا وَلَا
تَكُن مَّعَ ٱلۡكَٰفِرِينَ ﴿٤٢﴾ قَالَ سَـَٔاوِيٓ إِلَىٰ جَبَلٖ يَعۡصِمُنِي
مِنَ ٱلۡمَآءِۚ قَالَ لَا عَاصِمَ ٱلۡيَوۡمَ مِنۡ أَمۡرِ ٱللَّهِ إِلَّا مَن رَّحِمَۚ
وَحَالَ بَيۡنَهُمَا ٱلۡمَوۡجُ فَكَانَ مِنَ ٱلۡمُغۡرَقِينَ ﴿٤٣﴾ وَقِيلَ
يَٰٓأَرۡضُ ٱبۡلَعِي مَآءَكِ وَيَٰسَمَآءُ أَقۡلِعِي وَغِيضَ ٱلۡمَآءُ وَقُضِيَ ٱلۡأَ
مۡرُ وَٱسۡتَوَتۡ عَلَى ٱلۡجُودِيِّۖ وَقِيلَ بُعۡدٗا لِّلۡقَوۡمِ ٱلظَّٰلِمِينَ ﴿٤٤﴾

And [Noah] said, "Embark therein; in the name of Allah is its course and its anchorage. Indeed, my Lord is Forgiving

---

translated by FaisalAl-Shafiq, Darrusalam, 2003

and Merciful." 41 And it sailed with them through waves like mountains, and Noah called to his son who was apart [from them], "O my son, come aboard with us and be not with the disbelievers." 42 [But] he said, "I will take refuge on a mountain to protect me from the water." [Noah] said, "There is no protector today from the decree of Allah, except for whom He gives mercy." And the waves came between them, and he was among the drowned. 43 And it was said, "O earth, swallow your water, and O sky, withhold [your rain]." And the water subsided, and the matter was accomplished, and the ship came to rest on the [mountain of] Judiyy. And it was said, "Away with the wrongdoing people." [194]

- Verse 45-47

وَنَادَىٰ نُوحٌ رَّبَّهُۥ فَقَالَ رَبِّ إِنَّ ٱبْنِى مِنْ أَهْلِى وَإِنَّ وَعْدَكَ
ٱلْحَقُّ وَأَنتَ أَحْكَمُ ٱلْحَٰكِمِينَ ﴿٤٥﴾

And Noah called to his Lord and said, "My Lord, indeed my son is of my family; and indeed, Your promise is true; and You are the most just of judges!" [195]

قَالَ يَٰنُوحُ إِنَّهُۥ لَيْسَ مِنْ أَهْلِكَ ۖ إِنَّهُۥ عَمَلٌ غَيْرُ صَٰلِحٍ ۖ فَلَا تَسْـَٔلْنِ مَا
لَيْسَ لَكَ بِهِۦ عِلْمٌ ۖ إِنِّىٓ أَعِظُكَ أَن تَكُونَ مِنَ ٱلْجَٰهِلِينَ ﴿٤٦﴾
قَالَ رَبِّ إِنِّىٓ أَعُوذُ بِكَ أَنْ أَسْـَٔلَكَ مَا لَيْسَ لِى بِهِۦ عِلْمٌ ۖ وَإِلَّا
تَغْفِرْ لِى وَتَرْحَمْنِىٓ أَكُن مِّنَ ٱلْخَٰسِرِينَ ﴿٤٧﴾

He said, "O Noah, indeed he is not of your family; indeed, he is [one whose] work was other than righteous, so ask Me not for

194. Hud, Ayah 41- 44
195. Hud, Ayah 45

that about which you have no knowledge. Indeed, I advise you, lest you be among the ignorant." [196]

[Noah] said, "My Lord, I seek refuge in You from asking that of which I have no knowledge. And unless You forgive me and have mercy upon me, I will be among the losers." [197]

This Quranic passage, depicting the story of Nuh (Noah) and his son, highlights a crucial aspect of Islamic tarbiyah and its implementation. The story emphasizes that faith and morality form the foundation of Islamic upbringing, distinguishing it with unique characteristics and an effective and practical approach.

Key insights regarding the upbringing of a child's faith can be derived from this story:

- Nuh exerted his utmost effort to win his son's heart, despite the eventual rejection of the invitation to Tawheed (monotheism).
- Parents or guardians should not be overly concerned about the outcome, as it ultimately lies in the hands of Allah ﷻ, the Almighty.
- Nuh's son was among those whom Nuh tirelessly and wholeheartedly invited to believe in Allah ﷻ for a remarkable period of 950 years. This is a profound example of the boundless nature of time and the commitment required in tarbiyah and dawa (invitation to Islam).
- Patience plays a crucial role in the moral upbringing of children. Allah commands us to remain patient and steadfast

196. Hud 46
197. Hud, Ayah 47

when calling our children to prayer.

- As the Quran states:

وَأْمُرْ أَهْلَكَ بِالصَّلَوٰةِ وَاصْطَبِرْ عَلَيْهَا ۖ لَا نَسْـَٔلُكَ رِزْقًا ۖ نَّحْنُ نَرْزُقُكَ ۗ وَالْعَـٰقِبَةُ لِلتَّقْوَىٰ ﴿١٣٢﴾

"And enjoin prayer upon your family [and people] and be steadfast therein. We ask you not for provision; We provide for you, and the [best] outcome is for [those of] righteousness". [198]

From the story, we understand the distinctive principle that sets apart the Islamic perspective on relationships and connections. In Islam, what truly binds people together is not based on blood relations, family, land, country, tribe, nation, color, language, race, profession, or social class. Rather, it is faith in Allah and belief in His oneness that serves as the defining factor.

When Prophet Nuh appealed to Allah ﷻ to save his son Kan'an, assuming that their biological bond would be a sufficient reason, Allah ﷻ responded by emphasizing that Kan'an could no longer be considered part of Nuh's family due to his unrighteous conduct and lack of faith. The tie of faith truly unites individuals within the Islamic framework.

The unique bond of the Islamic faith is rooted in specific objectives and aspirations outlined by divine guidance. It surpasses otherworldly connections, as they can be severed despite the existence of various ties.

198. Ta-Ha, Ayah 132

"The tie which binds people together in the Islamic faith is unique. It relates to certain objectives and aspirations which are peculiar to this divine constitution. This tie of Islamic society has nothing to do with family or blood relations, land or country, tribe or nation, color or language, race or sex, profession or class. All such ties may exist between two individuals, yet their relations may, nevertheless, still be severed."[199]

Islam emphasizes that the strongest bond between individuals lies in their shared faith and commitment to Allah, transcending any other worldly affiliations.

C. Ibrahim and his sons:

The moral upbringing code in verses 37 of surat ibrahim, verses 131-133 of surat al-baqrah, and verses 100-106 of surat al-safat: (ibrahim and his sons)

- VERSE 37

Allah ﷻ says in surat Ibrahim:

رَّبَّنَآ إِنِّيٓ أَسۡكَنتُ مِن ذُرِّيَّتِي بِوَادٍ غَيۡرِ ذِي زَرۡعٍ عِندَ بَيۡتِكَ
ٱلۡمُحَرَّمِ رَبَّنَا لِيُقِيمُواْ ٱلصَّلَوٰةَ فَٱجۡعَلۡ أَفۡـِٔدَةٗ مِّنَ ٱلنَّاسِ
تَهۡوِيٓ إِلَيۡهِمۡ وَٱرۡزُقۡهُم مِّنَ ٱلثَّمَرَٰتِ لَعَلَّهُمۡ يَشۡكُرُونَ ٣٧

"Our Lord, I have settled some of my descendants in an uncultivated valley near Your sacred House, our Lord, that they may establish prayer. So make hearts among the people

199. Zilal al-Quran, an online Tafseer (interpretation), on page 192 of Surat Hud

incline toward them and provide for them from the fruits that they might be grateful". [200]

- Verses 131-133

In surat Al-Baqrah, Allah says:

إِذۡ قَالَ لَهُۥ رَبُّهُۥٓ أَسۡلِمۡۖ قَالَ أَسۡلَمۡتُ لِرَبِّ ٱلۡعَٰلَمِينَ ١٣١
وَوَصَّىٰ بِهَآ إِبۡرَٰهِـۧمُ بَنِيهِ وَيَعۡقُوبُ يَٰبَنِيَّ إِنَّ ٱللَّهَ ٱصۡطَفَىٰ لَكُمُ
ٱلدِّينَ فَلَا تَمُوتُنَّ إِلَّا وَأَنتُم مُّسۡلِمُونَ ١٣٢ أَمۡ كُنتُمۡ شُهَدَآءَ
إِذۡ حَضَرَ يَعۡقُوبَ ٱلۡمَوۡتُ إِذۡ قَالَ لِبَنِيهِ مَا تَعۡبُدُونَ مِنۢ
بَعۡدِيۖ قَالُواْ نَعۡبُدُ إِلَٰهَكَ وَإِلَٰهَ ءَابَآئِكَ إِبۡرَٰهِـۧمَ وَإِسۡمَٰعِيلَ
وَإِسۡحَٰقَ إِلَٰهٗا وَٰحِدٗا وَنَحۡنُ لَهُۥ مُسۡلِمُونَ ١٣٣

When his Lord said to him, "Submit", he said "I have submitted [in Islam] to the Lord of the worlds."

And Abraham instructed his sons [to do the same] and [so did] Jacob, [saying], "O my sons, indeed Allah has chosen for you this religion, so do not die except while you are Muslims."

"Or were you witnesses when death approached Jacob, when he said to his sons, "What will you worship after me?" They said, "We will worship your God and the God of your fathers, Abraham and Ishmael and Isaac - one God. And we are Muslims [in submission] to Him." [201]

200. Ibrahim, Ayah 37
201. Al-baqrah 131-133

- Verses 100-106

رَبِّ هَبْ لِى مِنَ ٱلصَّٰلِحِينَ ﴿١٠٠﴾ فَبَشَّرْنَٰهُ بِغُلَٰمٍ حَلِيمٍ ﴿١٠١﴾
فَلَمَّا بَلَغَ مَعَهُ ٱلسَّعْىَ قَالَ يَٰبُنَىَّ إِنِّىٓ أَرَىٰ فِى ٱلْمَنَامِ أَنِّىٓ أَذْبَحُكَ
فَٱنظُرْ مَاذَا تَرَىٰ ۚ قَالَ يَٰٓأَبَتِ ٱفْعَلْ مَا تُؤْمَرُ ۖ سَتَجِدُنِىٓ إِن شَآءَ
ٱللَّهُ مِنَ ٱلصَّٰبِرِينَ ﴿١٠٢﴾ فَلَمَّآ أَسْلَمَا وَتَلَّهُۥ لِلْجَبِينِ ﴿١٠٣﴾
وَنَٰدَيْنَٰهُ أَن يَٰٓإِبْرَٰهِيمُ ﴿١٠٤﴾ قَدْ صَدَّقْتَ ٱلرُّءْيَآ ۚ إِنَّا كَذَٰلِكَ نَجْزِى
ٱلْمُحْسِنِينَ ﴿١٠٥﴾ إِنَّ هَٰذَا لَهُوَ ٱلْبَلَٰٓؤُا۟ ٱلْمُبِينُ ﴿١٠٦﴾

> "My Lord, grant me [a child] from among the righteous." So We gave him good tidings of a forbearing boy. And when he reached with him [the age of] exertion, he said, "O my son, indeed I have seen in a dream that I [must] sacrifice you, so see what you think." He said, "O my father, do as you are commanded. You will find me, if Allah wills, of the steadfast." And when they had both submitted and he put him down upon his forehead, We called to him, "O Abraham, You have fulfilled the vision." Indeed, We thus reward the doers of good. Indeed, this was the clear trial». [202]

Verse 37 of Surat Ibrahim provides valuable lessons about successful parenting and the devotion required when raising children with strong moral values. From the story of Prophet Ibrahim and his family, we can learn the following essential principles of tarbiyah:

- The utmost fairness is required. Children's obedience to their parents is closely tied to the parents' obedience to Allah. When Allah tested Prophet Ibrahim by instructing him to leave

202. As-Saaffat, Ayah 103-106

his wife Hajirah and son Ismael in the open desert, Ibrahim obeyed without complaint. His wife asked if it was his decision or a command from Allah ﷻ, to which she responded that Allah ﷻ would take care of them and never neglect them. This teaches parents that relying on Allah ﷻ is crucial in raising their children. When parents obey Allah, they set an example for their children.

- Prophet Ibrahim's primary concern was the faith and religiosity of his family. He prioritized their devotion to Allah ﷻ and the establishment of prayers in the house of Allah. This highlights an important lesson for parents who seek to raise their children with a strong religious foundation. Creating a conducive environment where children can worship Allah and maintain their Islamic identity is essential for their upbringing.
- Hajirah, the wife of Ibrahim, provides a particular lesson for mothers on how to raise a child alone without the support of a husband or family. Despite enduring all the hardships alone, she raised a dutiful child to Allah, who obeyed his father. She nurtured Ismael with utmost care and manners. This is a powerful and practical lesson of tarbiyah for single parents, whether fathers or mothers, who are raising their children alone.

Verse 37 of Surat Ibrahim offers valuable insights into successful parenting. It emphasizes the importance of parents' obedience to Allah, the priority of nurturing a child's faith and religiosity, and the ability to raise children alone with dedication and care. These lessons serve as guidance for parents striving to raise their children in accordance with Islamic values.

Furthermore, in verses 131-133 of Surat Al-Baqarah, we gain important insights:

- The journey of Tarbiyah, or nurturing and upbringing, extends throughout one's entire life. This serves as a lesson for parents to remain committed to the Tarbiyah curriculum they instill in their children, recognizing that the process continues until their own death.
- Following the teachings of his father Ibrahim, Prophet Yakub conveyed the message of Tawheed (the belief in the oneness of Allah) to his children on his deathbed. This is a practical lesson for Muslim parents, highlighting the significance of raising their children with a strong foundation in Tawheed. Tawheed should be at the core of their Tarbiyah efforts.
- Like his father before him, Prophet Yakub was deeply concerned about his children's worship of Allah alone and their adherence to the path of monotheism. This highlights the goal that every Muslim parent should strive for to ensure their children die as pure Muslims, firmly grounded in the belief in the oneness of Allah ﷻ. Parents should prioritize this objective before they depart from this world.
- It is incumbent upon parents to pass on the legacy of Tawheed to their children, ensuring that the belief in the oneness of Allah ﷻ resonates in future generations. This emphasizes the importance of transmitting the teachings of Tawheed to succeeding generations, ensuring its continuity and impact.

In conclusion, verses 131-133 of Surat Al-Baqarah provide valuable lessons for parents. They underscore the lifelong nature of the Tarbiyah journey, the importance of raising children on the foundation of Tawheed, the significance of parents' concern for their children's faith, and the duty of passing on the legacy of Tawheed to future generations. By internalizing these lessons, parents can strive to raise their children upon the principles of Tawheed, ensuring a strong and lasting connection with Allah ﷻ throughout their lives.

- Regarding verses 103-106 of Surat Al-Saffat, we can derive several significant lessons from Prophet Ismail's readiness to obey the command of Allah as conveyed by his father, Prophet Ibrahim:

- Prophet Ismail's remarkable maturity is evident despite his young age. His immediate acceptance and obedience to Allah's command showcase his deep understanding and devotion.

- This obedience and maturity could not have been achieved without his parents' guidance and successful upbringing. It emphasizes parents' crucial role in raising obedient and morally nurtured children who have a strong connection with Allah ﷻ and their parents. Ismail's beautiful response, "O my father, do as you are commanded. You will find me if Allah wills, of the steadfast," exemplifies the essence of true obedience.

- Prophet Ibrahim's effective and successful guidance of his son was rooted in divine revelation. This highlights the importance of effective communication between parents and children in fostering a positive upbringing.

- Prophet Ibrahim's approach to addressing his son as "Ya Bunayya," which conveys affection and endearment, reflects his loving and gentle manner of dealing with his son. Instead of relying on authority and power, Ibrahim approached his son with good manners, love, and affection.
- In the previous verse (102), Prophet Ibrahim's consultative approach with his son, saying, "So see what you think," emphasizes the importance of avoiding authoritarianism and empowering children to make decisions about their own lives. This approach helps build their personality, cultivate confidence, and foster independence.
- The Quran acknowledges that the incident served as a test of faith for both Prophet Ibrahim and Ismail, examining their obedience to Allah despite their hardships and challenges. This highlights the concept that tests and evaluations, not limited to formal education, can be used by parents as tools for character-building and developing their children's potential. Challenging tasks and assessments can be employed methodologically to uplift and elevate children's character and test their resilience.

In conclusion, verses 103-106 of Surat Al-Saffat offer valuable lessons for parents. They highlight the importance of nurturing obedience and moral values in children, emphasizing the role of parents in providing guidance and instilling a strong connection with Allah ﷻ. These verses also underscore the significance of effective communication, love, and affection in parent-child relationships and the value of empowering children and utilizing tests and assessments as tools for character development. By incorporating these lessons into their parenting approach, parents can raise obedient, morally upright, and resilient children in their faith.[203]

D. Yakub and his sons:

the moral upbringing code in verses 3-4, 13, 67, and 97-98 of surat yusuf. (yakub and his sons)

Verses 3-4

إِذْ قَالَ يُوسُفُ لِأَبِيهِ يَٰٓأَبَتِ إِنِّي رَأَيْتُ أَحَدَ عَشَرَ كَوْكَبًا وَٱلشَّمْسَ
وَٱلْقَمَرَ رَأَيْتُهُمْ لِي سَٰجِدِينَ ٤ قَالَ يَٰبُنَيَّ لَا تَقْصُصْ رُءْيَا
كَ عَلَىٰٓ إِخْوَتِكَ فَيَكِيدُوا۟ لَكَ كَيْدًا إِنَّ ٱلشَّيْطَٰنَ لِلْإِنسَٰنِ عَدُوٌّ
مُّبِينٌ ٥

[Of these stories mention] when Joseph said to his father, "O my father, indeed I have seen [in a dream] eleven stars and the sun and the moon; I saw them prostrating to me." He said, "O my son, do not relate your vision to your brothers or they will contrive against you a plan. Indeed Satan, to man, is a manifest enemy".[204]

Verse 12- 13

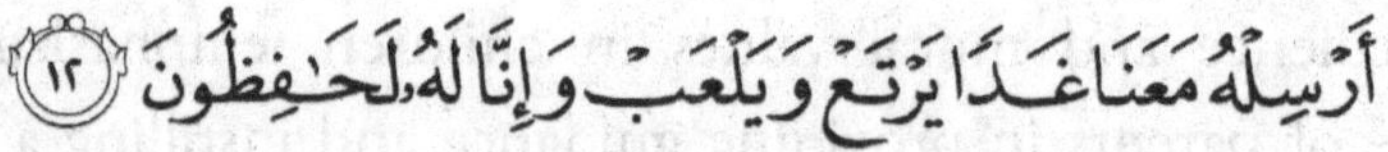

203. Dr. Muhamad Hanif Hassan. Powerful conversations between a father and a son: lessons from Ibrahim and Prophet Ismail As. 19/7/2021
204. Yusuf, Ayah 4- 5

قَالَ إِنِّي لَيَحْزُنُنِيٓ أَن تَذْهَبُواْ بِهِۦ وَأَخَافُ أَن يَأْكُلَهُ ٱلذِّئْبُ
وَأَنتُمْ عَنْهُ غَٰفِلُونَ ١٣

"Send him with us tomorrow that he may eat well and play. And indeed, we will be his guardians.

[Jacob] said, "Indeed, it saddens me that you should take him, and I fear that a wolf would eat him while you are of him unaware." [205]

Verse 67

وَقَالَ يَٰبَنِيَّ لَا تَدْخُلُواْ مِنۢ بَابٖ وَٰحِدٖ وَٱدْخُلُواْ مِنْ أَبْوَٰبٖ مُّتَفَرِّقَةٖۖ
وَمَآ أُغْنِي عَنكُم مِّنَ ٱللَّهِ مِن شَيْءٍۖ إِنِ ٱلْحُكْمُ إِلَّا لِلَّهِۖ عَلَيْهِ تَوَ
كَّلْتُۖ وَعَلَيْهِ فَلْيَتَوَكَّلِ ٱلْمُتَوَكِّلُونَ ٦٧

"And he said, "O my sons, do not enter from one gate but enter from different gates; and I cannot avail you against [the decree of] Allah at all. The decision is only for Allah ; upon Him I have relied, and upon Him let those who would rely [indeed] rely." [206]

Verses 97-98

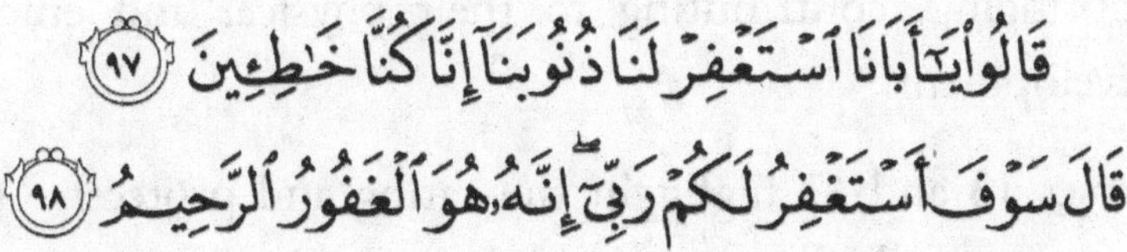

"They said, "O our father, ask for us forgiveness of our sins; indeed, we have been sinners." He said, "I will ask forgiveness

205. Yusuf, Ayah 12 – 13
206. Yusuf, Ayah 67

for you from my Lord. Indeed, it is He who is the Forgiving, the Merciful."[207]

Surat Yusuf contains many historical episodes, but this writing focuses on the parent-child relations depicted in the surah. The following aspects can be learned from the surah:

- Verses 3-4 highlight the strong bond between Yusuf and his father, Yakub. This close relationship was cultivated through Yakub's nurturing of his son, fostering an environment of trust and friendship where Yusuf felt comfortable sharing his secrets and dreams with his father. Such a friendship between parent and child leaves a lasting impact on their character and facilitates the parent's ability to closely attend to their child's moral well-being.

- Verse 12, mentioning the word "play," emphasizes the importance of allowing children to experience and enjoy their childhood. Play is a crucial source of learning basic social morals and skills necessary for life, and it should be valued as an essential aspect of a child's character-building and personality development. Allowing children to play is integral to their upbringing, contributing to their physical and emotional development.

- Verses 13 and 67 highlight the caring and protective nature parents should have towards their children's security, well-being, and safety. Yakub expresses his sadness and concern when his child is exposed to potentially dangerous situations, such as being vulnerable to wolves, in verse 13. Similarly, in verse 67,

207. Yusuf, Ayah 97 - 98

Yakub advises his sons to enter the town through separate gates to protect them from the evil eye, envy, suspicion, or any other potential harm. This demonstrates the parental responsibility to ensure the safety and protection of their children.

- Verses 97-98 teach parents the importance of forgiveness and praying for their children. Despite Yusuf's siblings' grave mistakes of mistreating him out of jealousy, neither Yusuf nor their father reminds them of their past failures. Constantly reminding a child of their past mistakes can have negative effects and potentially encourage them to repeat those mistakes. Opening a new chapter for a child after they make mistakes, without dwelling on the past, can foster self-confidence and motivate them to make better choices in the future.

In conclusion, Surat Yusuf provides valuable insights into parent-child relationships. It emphasizes the importance of building a strong bond of friendship, allowing children to enjoy their childhood through play, prioritizing the safety and protection of children, and practicing forgiveness while guiding them toward personal growth. By reflecting on these lessons, parents can strive to create a nurturing and supportive environment for their children's holistic development.

3.2 Righteousness of parents:

The moral upbringing code in verses 9 of surat al-nisa, 82 of surat al-kahf, and 21 of surat al-tur. (righteousness of parents and its influence on their offspring):

The purpose of nurturing children with good morals and etiquette is to guide them and foster a strong connection with their Creator, the Almighty, to seek His pleasure and attain success and prosperity in their lives. Upon reflecting on various Quranic verses, one can infer that through the parents' righteousness, Allah ﷻ bestows upon their offspring care, blessings, success, protection, and salvation from the torment of hell in the hereafter. Three verses in the Quran, found in different chapters, implicitly and explicitly demonstrate how the piety and righteousness of parents can benefit their children and lead them to success in all aspects of their lives. The following are the three verses, along with their explanations:

- In Surat Al-Nisa, Allah ﷻ says:

وَلْيَخْشَ ٱلَّذِينَ لَوْ تَرَكُوا۟ مِنْ خَلْفِهِمْ ذُرِّيَّةً ضِعَٰفًا خَافُوا۟

عَلَيْهِمْ فَلْيَتَّقُوا۟ ٱللَّهَ وَلْيَقُولُوا۟ قَوْلًا سَدِيدًا ٩

"And let those [executors and guardians] fear [injustice] as if they [themselves] had left weak offspring behind and feared for them. So let them fear Allah and speak words of appropriate justice". 208

- In surat Al-Kahf, the verse reads as follows:

وَكَانَ تَحْتَهُۥ كَنزٌ لَّهُمَا وَكَانَ أَبُوهُمَا صَٰلِحًا

"And their father had been righteous" 209

- Allah ﷻ said in surat Al-Tur:

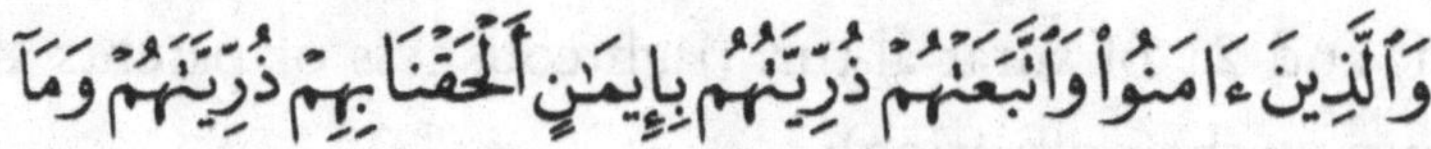

208. Al-Nisa vers 9
209. Al-kaf 82

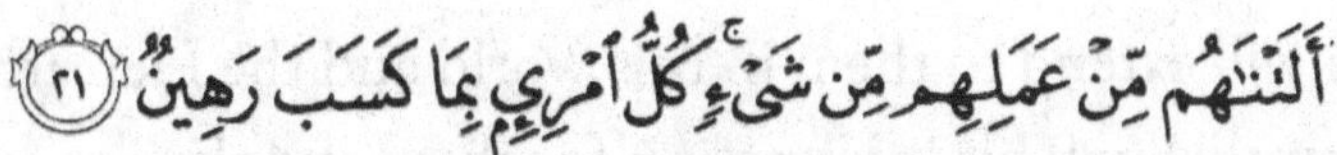

"And those who believed and whose descendants followed them in faith - We will join with them their descendants, and We will not deprive them of anything of their deeds. Every person, for what he earned, is retained". [210]

- In his comments on verse 9 of al-nisa al-Qusheiry says: "It is proven in this verse that what a Muslim should save for his children is piety and righteousness, not money. Because Allah did ask the parents to collect money, build many houses, or leave them a piece of furniture. All that Allah asked them for was to fear Him, and He will take care of them by being righteous".[211]

At the end of the verse, it states, "So let them fear Allah and speak words of appropriate justice," which demonstrates that the parent's adherence to the teachings of Islam in terms of his/her word "being just and truthteller" and action " being God-conscious" can be helpful to the offspring and secure their life and well-being during and after the parent's life. Al-Qusheyr's comment on the verse is well-said that the best legacy of a parent to his/her offspring is righteousness instead of money, Real-states, or any other worldly material which people take pride in its possession.

Ibnu Katheer elaborating on verse 82 of al-kahf, said: وكان أبوهما صالحا)

Their father was a righteous man) indicates that a righteous person's offspring will be taken care of and that the blessing of his

210. At-Tur, Ayah 21
211. Al-Kusheiry, Lata'If Al-Isharat vol: page: 316.

worship will extend to them in this world and the Hereafter. This will occur through his intercession for them and their status being raised to the highest levels of Paradise so that he may find joy in them. This was stated in the Qur'an and reported in the Sunnah. Sa`id bin Jubayr narrated from Ibn `Abbas: "They were taken care of because their father was a righteous man, although it is not stated that they were righteous."[212]

It also reads in Maarif ul-Quran that: "Muhammad ibn al-Munkadir says: 'It is because of the piety and righteousness of a servant of His that Allah Ta' ala protects his children, and the children of his children, and his family, even the homes built around his own.'"[213]

Added to the illustrations in verse is that of Al-Qurtubi, where he said in his Tafseer: "The verse indicates that Allah ﷻ, the Almighty, preserves the righteous in himself, his children, and his grandchildren. It was narrated that Allah, the Almighty, preserves the righteous in seven of his offspring, And this is evidenced by His saying- the Almighty: Indeed my protector is Allah, who has sent down the book; and He is an ally to the righteous (protects him)."[214]

Allah ﷻ promises to care for the offspring of His servants and provide them protection when the servant demonstrates commitment and wholeheartedly follows the teachings of Allah ﷻ in their words and actions. By being devout and dedicated to

212. Tafseer ibn katheer vol: 6 page 185

213. (Mazhari) Al-A'raf 196. Maarif ul-Quran and Tafseer Al-Qurtubi vol: 10 page: 407

214. Al-A'raf 196. Tafseer Al-Qurtubi vol: 10 pages: 407

their faith, individuals can ensure the well-being and safeguarding of their children.

- Regarding Verse 21 of Al-Tur, as explained by renowned Quran commentators like Ibnu Katheer and others, it emphasizes that if righteous parents serve as role models for their children in matters of faith and piety, Allah, in the hereafter, rewards the parents by elevating their children to the same rank as them. Consequently, they will all be united in Paradise. Ibnu Katheer provides the following quotation to support this interpretation:

"In this Ayah, Allah the Exalted affirms His favor, generosity, graciousness, compassion, and beneficence towards His creation. When the offspring of the righteous believers imitate their parents regarding faith, Allah will elevate the latter to the ranks of the former, even though the latter did not perform deeds as goodly as their parents. Allah will comfort the eyes of the parents by seeing their offspring elevated in their grades. Indeed, Allah will gather them together in the best manner, and He will not decrease the reward or the grades of those higher in rank for joining them together, hence His statement, "To them shall We join their offspring, and We shall not decrease the reward of their deeds in anything.) Ath-Thawri reported that Amr ibn Murah said that Said bin Jubeir said that Ibn `Abbas said, "Verily, Allah elevates the ranks of the believers' offspring to the rank of their parents, even though the latter has not performed as well as the former so that the eyes of the parents are comforted." Ibn `Abbas then recited this Ayah (And those who believe and whose offspring follow them in faith, -- to them shall We join their offspring.) saying, "They are the offspring of the believers who died on the faith. If their parents' ranks are higher than theirs, they will be joined with their parents. No part of the reward their parents received for their good deeds will be reduced for them.' [215]

3.3 Child disciplining:

The Moral Upbringing Code in Verse 58 of Al-Nur "The Optimal Time to Begin Disciplining a Child"

Allah ﷻ says:

يَـٰٓأَيُّهَا ٱلَّذِينَ ءَامَنُوا۟ لِيَسْتَـْٔذِنكُمُ ٱلَّذِينَ مَلَكَتْ أَيْمَـٰنُكُمْ وَٱلَّذِينَ
لَمْ يَبْلُغُوا۟ ٱلْحُلُمَ مِنكُمْ ثَلَـٰثَ مَرَّٰتٍ ۚ مِّن قَبْلِ صَلَوٰةِ ٱلْفَجْرِ وَحِينَ تَضَعُونَ
ثِيَابَكُم مِّنَ ٱلظَّهِيرَةِ وَمِنۢ بَعْدِ صَلَوٰةِ ٱلْعِشَآءِ ۚ ثَلَـٰثُ عَوْرَٰتٍ لَّكُمْ ۚ
لَيْسَ عَلَيْكُمْ وَلَا عَلَيْهِمْ جُنَاحٌۢ بَعْدَهُنَّ ۚ طَوَّٰفُونَ عَلَيْكُم
بَعْضُكُمْ عَلَىٰ بَعْضٍ ۚ كَذَٰلِكَ يُبَيِّنُ ٱللَّهُ لَكُمُ ٱلْـَٔايَـٰتِ ۗ وَٱللَّهُ عَلِيمٌ
حَكِيمٌ ﴿٥٨﴾

"O you who have believed, let those whom your right hands possess and those who have not [yet] reached puberty among you ask permission of you [before entering] at three times: before the dawn prayer and when you put aside your clothing [for rest] at noon and after the night prayer. [These are] three times of privacy for you. There is no blame upon you nor upon them beyond these [periods], for they continually circulate

215. Ibn Katheer vol: 13 pages: 232

> among you - some of you, among others. Thus does Allah make clear to you the verses; and Allah is Knowing and Wise". [216]

In verse above, "Let those who have not [yet] reached puberty among you ask permission of you [before entering]," it instructs the parents on the right time when they should start teaching their children the basic etiquette of Islam, such as asking permission before entering the house because of privacy.

At this early stage (middle childhood), and the age when the child has the conscience to perceive and distinguish between right and wrong and simultaneously understand the instructions given to him by the parent is when it is highly recommended to raise the child on morals, manners, and etiquettes of Islam.

It is, undoubtedly, the proper and the most fitting stage to morally prepare them. That is why shari'a encourages the parents to consider starting nurturing the child at this very stage because of the easiness of molding and shaping the children in this period.

Accordingly, the prophet, peace upon him, commands the believers to order their children to pray at the age of seven so that the prayer becomes the first step of the child's connection with Allah ﷻ;

Amr bin Shu'aib reported on his father's authority that his grandfather رضي الله عنه said that the messenger of Allah ﷺ said:

« مروا أولادكم بالصلاة وهم أبناء سبع سنين .. »

"Command your children to perform Salat (prayer) when they are seven years old."[217]

216. An-Nur 58
217. Abu Daud Al-Sunan, Hadith, No: 496, Ahmed, Al-Musnad 6689.

The childhood period, from birth to age eight, is crucial for instilling discipline and cultivating desirable qualities in children. This is a period when children are like sponges, eagerly absorbing everything their parents show, teach, and tell them. During this time, parents have significant influence over their children's development. It is essential for parents to nurture their children, shaping them into individuals that align with their aspirations.

According to Shahid Athar's article "Influencing the Behavior of Muslim Youth and their Parents," parents strongly influence their children, especially during the early years (0-8 years), accounting for up to 80% of their influence. However, as children grow, they begin to explore new friendships and encounter diverse ideas, which gradually make them independent from the sole influence of their parents.

Likewise, around the age of seven, children start displaying a natural inclination towards logical reasoning and developing an understanding of Islamic ethics. Their constant and inquisitive questioning about their surroundings, whether it be what they see, hear, think, or even imagine, indicates their readiness to receive instruction and guidance.

Children possess a remarkable receptivity to various influences. As described by Athar, "They are like molten cement, easily molded by anything that falls upon them, leaving lasting impressions." Their minds resemble untouched soil, eager to accept any seed planted within.

As they mature, their ability to absorb new ideas and influences expands. We must filter the experiential factors that shape a child's development, ensuring they embrace positive ideas and behaviors while rejecting negative influences.[218]

Furthermore, Ibnul Qayim emphasized the paramount importance of nurturing children and instilling them with good moral conduct during their formative years. He stated: "One of the most urgent needs of a child is close attention to their moral well-being. They grow up influenced by the habits and behaviors they are accustomed to in their early years. If they are exposed to resentment, anger, arguments, impatience, succumbing to whims and desires, foolishness, a quick temper, and greed, it will be challenging for them to change these traits as they grow older. Consequently, we find that many people have deviant characters due to their upbringing." [219]

In conclusion, the Islamic perspective highlights several essential principles that are crucial to parent-child relationships. The extensive discussion and analysis of Quranic verses in this context clearly demonstrate that parents play a vital role in shaping their children's mindset, attitudes, moral standards, and overall strength and positivity.

Hence, if parents strive to their utmost ability, serving as role models for their children's moral conduct and raising them with righteousness to safeguard them from the perils of hellfire, as commanded by Allah in verse 6 of Surat Al-Tahreem, they will ultimately succeed in nurturing a morally upright generation

218. ibid.
219. Ibnul Qayim, Tuhfatul Mowluud 240

capable of making significant and positive contributions to Islam and humanity as a whole. However, to realize this vision, parents must approach this task with seriousness, sincerity, and a genuine commitment to displaying impeccable virtues and moral conduct that will shape their children's character and overall personality.

REFERENCES

Books

Abdal-Wahab, AlKadi Abi Muhammad. n.d. *Al-Talqeen Fi Al-Fiqh Al-Maliki.* Dar Al-Kutub Al-'Ilmiyyah.

ad-Dimishqi, Isma'il bin Umar ibn Kathir. 2003. *Tafsir Ibn Kathir Tafsir Al-Qur'anil 'Adheem.* Riyad: Darussalam, Darul feyha.

al-Baghaw, bū Muḥammad al-Ḥusayn ibn Mas'ūd ibn Muḥammad al-Farrā'. 1983. *SHARH AS-SUNNAH BY IMAM AL-BAGHAWI.* Damascus.

al-Bayhaqi, Abu Bakr Ahmad ibn al-Husain. 1994. *Sunan al-Kubra* . Beirut: Dar Al-Kotob Al-Ilmiyah.

Al-Bukhari, Imam. 1996. *Sahih Al-Bukhari.* Riyad: Maktaba Dar-us-Salam.

Al-deen, Al-Albani Muhammad Nasir. 2000. *At-Targheeb wat-Tarheeb.* Riyad: Dar Al Maarifah.

Al-deen, Al-Albani Muhammad Nasir. 2001. *Sahih Al-Adab al-Mufrad* . Darul Sadiqin.

—. 2004. *Silsilaat Al-Ahadith Al-Sahihah.* Riyad: Dar Al Maarifah.

Al-Ghazali, Abu Hamid. 2020. *Iḥyā ulūm al-dīn.* London: Turath Publishing.

AL-JAZA'IRY, SHAYKH ABU BAKR JABIR. 2001. *MINHAJ AL-MUSLIM.* Riyad: Darussalam publishers.

al-Qazvini, Muhammad bin Yazid Ibn Majah. n.d. *Sunan ibn Majah.*

al-Qurtubi, Abu Abdullah Muhammad ibn Ahmad. n.d. *TAFSIR AL-QURTUBI - AL-JAMI' LI AHKAM AL-QURAN.* Darul Kitab Al-Ararabi.

Al-Razi, Imam Fakhr Al-din. n.d. *Al-Tafsir Al-Kabir Aw Mafatih al-Ghaib.* Dar Kotob al-Ilmiyah.

Al-Suyuti, Al-Mahalli and. 2010. *Tafsir Al-Jalalayn.* Al Bushra Library.

as-Sijistan, Abu Dawud Sulayman ibn al-Ash'ath. n.d. *Sunan Abi Dawud.* Riyad: Dar Al Maarifah.

as-Suyūṭī, Imām Jalāl ad-Dīn. 1993. *Miftāḥ al-Jannah fī al-Iḥtijāj bi as-Sunnah.* Dar al-Nafa'is.

at-Tabari, Abu Ja'far Muhammad ibn Jarir. n.d. *TAFSIR IBN JARIR AT-TABARI - JAMI' AL-BAYAN 'AN TA-WIL AL-QURAN.* Dar Kotob Al-Ilmiyah.

at-Tirmidhi, Muhammad ibn 'Issa. 1978. *SUNAN AT-TIRMIDHI.* Beirut: Darul Fikr.

Az-Zuhayli, Wahbah. 2008. *Al-Fiqh Al-Shafi'i Al-Muyassar.* Damascus: Darul Fikr.

Guezzou, Mokrane. 2008. *Tafsir Ibn Abbas.* Louisville: Fons Vitae.

Ibn Hajar, Ahmed Bin Ali Bin Hajar. n.d. *Fathul Bari Sharah Sahihul Bukhari.* Beirut: Dar Al Maarifah.

Ibn Taymiyah, Taqi Ad-Deen Ahmed, 1997. *majmual fatawa.* Riyad: Daeul Wafa.

Majah, Ibn. n.d. *Sunan Ibn Majah.* Riyad: Darul Maarifah.

Mashood, Dr. Busari. 2017. "Iddat-talaq and iddat wafat: A reinterpretation of the phrase 'Hatta yada'na hamlahuna.'"

MAUDUDI, ABUL A'LA. n.d. *TAFHIM-UL-QURAN.*

Nawawi, Imam. 2003. *Riyad as-Salihin.* Darussalam.

Articles

Abdulsam, Dr. Sami. 2015. "ندب الحكمين في الخلع" "Empowering the arbitrators in the khula (divorce upon a settlement)." *London School of Economics and Political Science*, Juni 10.

Alaro, Dr. Abdul-Razzaq Abdul-Majeed. 2017. "Children Moral Upbringing: The Shariah Recipe." *Allawh Journal of Arabic and Islamic Studies, University of Maiduguri*, Juni 1.

Bakar, Naz. Abu. 1970. "Who represented the will of the people." *Council of Elders.*

Farooq, Sadaf. 2018. "Two Important Rules for a Blissful Marriage." August 22.

Hassan, Dr. Muhamad Hanif. 2021. "Powerful conversations between a father and a son: lessons from Ibrahim and prophet Ismail as." July 19

Josh McDowell, Don Stewart. 1983. "Handbook of Today's Religions." *Handbook of Today's Religions.*

Judith Bennett, Ruth Karras. 2013. *The Oxford Handbook of Women and Gender in Medieval Europe.* New York: Oxford University Press.

Muslim Skeptic Team. 2022. "Wife-beating" in Judaism, Christianity, Hinduism, Buddhism, and Islam." *Muslim Skeptic Team*, August 7

Refaat, Ayman. 2002. "Pleasing Allah through Taqwa. June." *AlJumuah Magazine*, June 27.

Reinhart, A. Kevin. 2017. "What We Know about Ma'ruf." *Journal of Islamic ethics.*

Shatibi, Ibrahim Ibn Musa Abu Ishaq Al. 2020. *Kitab Al-I'tisam.* Darul Affan.

Spiegel, James. 2010. "The Making of an Atheist." *The Making of an Atheist*, March 5.

Turner, Paul. n.d. "Finding your path arbitration sharia and the modern middle east."

Umm Mummad (Emily Assami), Mary Kennedy, Amatullah Bantley. 1997. *The Saheeh International translation.* The Publishing House (dar), dar Abul Qasim.

Waggoner, Jarl. 2022. "Responding Biblically to Atheism." *Responding Biblically to Atheism*, Juni 22.

Wardle, Lynn D. 2008. "The Morality of Marriage and the Transformative Power of Inclusion." September 1.

Internet

https://researchspace.ukzn.ac.za/handle/10413/7512
https://www.tibb.co.za/wp-content/uploads/2021/01/Medicine-of-the-prophet.pdf
https://archive.org/details/IBNASAKIRSREPRESENTATIONSOFSYRIAAND1/mode/2up
https://archive.org/details/in.ernet.dli.2015.431592/page/n3/mode/2up
https://archive.org/details/musnadahmadibnhanbal10/MusnadAhmadIbnHanbal10/
https://www.alim.org/quran/tafsir/ibn-kathir/
https://myislam.org/surah-yusuf/ayat-70/
https://quran.com/12:70/tafsirs/en-tafisr-ibn-kathir
https://www.kalamullah.com/Books/Ranks%20of%20the%20Divine%20Seekers%20vol%201.pdf
https://waqfeya.net/book.php?bid=3587

https://quran.com/12:70/tafsirs/en-tafsir-maarif-ul-quran
http://www.englishtafsir.com/
Kalamullah.Com | In the Shade of the Qur'an | Fi Dhilal al-Quran
Quran Tafsir | Tafsir Ibn Kathir - explanation of the Quran (alim.org)
Quranic Terminology: (Ilhad – Root: l/h/d) (ahl-alquran.com)
The Moral Space of Marriage in The Holy Quran – مركز خُطوة للتوثيق والدراسات (khotwacenter.com)
What We Know about Ma'rūf in: Journal of Islamic Ethics Volume 1 Issue 1-2 (2017) (brill.com)
Marital Harmony And Conflict Resolution: The Quranic Paradigm - MuslimMatters.org
Islamic perspective on Chilhood & Child protectiom (darul-ilm.co.uk)
Kindness to Parents (All parts) - The Religion of Islam (islamreligion.com)
Does the Quran let men beat their wives? (abuaminaelias.com)
Analyzing the so-called 'Wife Beating Verse': 4:34 of the Holy Quran - The Muslim Vibe
The Noble Quran - Quran.com
Kalamullah.Com | Quran | Ma'ariful Quran
https://islam4u.pro/blog/parents-in-quran/

www.ingramcontent.com/pod-product-compliance
Lightning Source LLC
LaVergne TN
LVHW031425170726
843492LV00009B/2859

* 9 7 8 8 2 6 9 3 6 7 7 0 6 *